REAL ESTATE
EDITION

MONEY
MATTERS

World's Leading Entrepreneurs Reveal their
TOP TIPS TO SUCCESS

ADAM TORRES AND
LUIS GUAJARDO

CENTURY CITY

Century City, CA

ENTER TO
WIN PRIZES
from *Money Matters* Top Tips

Scan the QR Code for entry into the contest.

WIN HERE

Follow Money Matters Top Tips to learn from other entrepreneurs, executives, and business owners on how to become a thought-leader in your field.

Podcast: **www.MoneyMattersTopTips.com/Podcast**
Instagram: **www.instagram.com/moneymatterstoptips**
Subscribe to the blog: **www.MoneyMattersTopTips.com**
Facebook: **www.facebook.com/moneymatterstoptips**
Twitter: **www.twitter.com/moneymatterstop**

Contest subject to terms and conditions listed on website.
No purchase necessary to participate.

For information, visit **www.MrCenturyCity.com**

Edited by:
Megan Kimble
Michael Douglas Carlin

Graphic Design:
Kendra Cagle

MONEY
M A T T E R S

CENTURY CITY

Century City, CA 90067
www.MrCenturyCity.com

The Mr. Century City Logo is a trademark of Mr. Century City, LLC.

ISBN 13: 978-1-949680-33-1

Money Matters, Beverly Hills, CA

DEDICATION

My friends and my family sometimes worked for free to help bring Prive into being. With their support, I have been through serious ups and downs. What we created together has now branched off into multiple companies and business models that complement each other. It all started in a small one-bedroom apartment in West Hollywood, booking vacation rentals for friends' houses in the Hollywood Hills while they traveled.

The company would not be where it is today without the support of all the people that pitched in, especially my brother, John Donikian, my mother, Yolanda Mendoza, who not only supported but also worked to help build Prive. I love you guys!

TABLE OF CONTENTS

ACKNOWLEDGEMENTS

I would like to thank the following individuals for their support and hard work throughout this effort.

Chirag Sagar COO of Destination Luxury

Victoria Kirk

Stella Song, CEO of Destination Luxury

Alice Yi, ESQ.

Michael Douglas Carlin, Editor - Century City News

Dr. Ben Shamoiel, The LA Chiropractor

Megan Kimble, Senior Editor

Kendra Cagle, 5 Lakes Design

Joe Casanova, Destination Luxury

Christopher Kai, KGL Consulting

Keyan Razi, CEO ImpactNEXT

Dan Bienenfeld, President of KERV Interactive

Matt Grey Ford, CEO of Urkli Marketing

FOREWORD

By **ADAM TORRES**

The loud banging on the steel security door of my 1-bedroom apartment in Phoenix, Arizona, woke me from a deep sleep. I looked at the alarm clock–it was 3 a.m. Someone was calling my name and it didn't sound like they were going away. Opening the door, I saw one of my tenants from Unit 3. He had an anxious look on his face. I knew this was going to be bad–no sleep tonight. He had family in town and, apparently, the bottom of the water heater in his apartment had rusted through. Water was flooding the entire apartment. At the moment, I thought–I didn't sign up for this when I purchased this building. Or had I?

My fascination with real estate started at a very young age. One of my earliest memories as a child, maybe around 4 years old, is of my father painting the side of our house. My rite of passage took place when I was 7 years old and was tasked to paint the inside of a hallway closet in a home my parents had just purchased. My scrawny arms held the brush and attempted to smoothly apply the paint while preventing drips from ruining my masterpiece. From that moment on, I was hooked.

My teenage years were spent soaking up every bit of knowledge I could about real estate and investing. Many teenagers view their driver's license as the ticket to freedom, allowing them to visit their friends and go to the mall at will. For me, getting my license allowed for my next rite of passage: securing two positions that would change my future. The first was working for a brokerage firm, Raymond James & Co; the second was working for a family that held significant real estate holdings. Instead of pursuing a schedule packed with sports and extracurricular activities, I wanted in to the world of finance. An average day for me during my junior and senior year of high school entailed going to classes from 8 a.m. to 11 a.m., working at the brokerage firm from 11:30 a.m. to 5 p.m., and then working in real estate from 6 p.m. to 10 p.m.

A lot has changed since those early experiences. Now with more than 12 years under my belt in finance, I've advised more than a thousand business owners. My work has spread to places as far away as Beijing, China, where I was hired to educate financial advisors. I've been quoted in publications such as *Forbes, Investor's Business Daily, U.S. News and World Report,* and *TheStreet.com*. I didn't play sports in high school. I never had the dream of making it to the NBA or NFL. For me, serving as an independent financial advisor in Century City, advising business owners, entrepreneurs, and executives, is the equivalent of making it to the NBA or NFL.

Though blessed to have obtained a certain measure of success, a couple of themes arose from my early experiences that I still live by today. These lessons are part of my inspiration for bringing you this book. The first lesson is to learn from people with a track record of success. When I worked at Raymond James & Co., my mentors had been in the industry for many years and had experienced multiple market cycles. The experiences they shared with me were invaluable and helped with my development as a financial advisor.

The real estate company I worked for had successfully acquired significant real estate holdings, and I got to see how they managed them in real time. I wasn't learning from people who were talking in abstract about real estate or finance theory. Instead, I saw first-hand applications of what happens when things go good and bad when assembling and managing a large portfolio of real estate holdings.

The second lesson, that is still relevant today, was how I reacted to new information. Often, we bring our own preconceived ideas into a learning opportunity which hinder our ability to take full advantage of the experience. I was lucky to start young—I was a blank slate and learning the language of finance from accomplished professionals. But what happens if you start later in life—is it too late to learn and incorporate new ideas? No, it's definitely not. Additional effort will be required to change current ideas you hold that might eventually turn out to be incorrect. The trouble emerges when you don't know you are incorrect—and when you're unwilling to listen to new ideas. As a rule of thumb, do more listening than talking when you are working with someone who has accomplished what you aim to do. Self-evaluation and maintaining an open mind are vital.

In putting together this book for you, I have stayed true to these two lessons. I assembled a group of professionals, who are accomplished in their respective fields, for you to learn from. Many have more than 20 years of experience, earning them the rank and status of accomplished entrepreneurs. This book is not focused on theory. Instead, it is a compilation of practical knowledge earned through real world experience in the real estate industry. It is a guide taught by the entrepreneurs that have the scars and accolades to prove their merit. The combined experience of the authors in this book is more than 250 years.

The second lesson is out of my control. How open you are, to the information given, is your decision. The authors assembled in this book truly are a special bunch. Originally, I created this platform for others to learn from. However, something unexpected happened as this book neared completion: As I read and approved each chapter's content, I realized how much I was learning. This was an unexpected personal benefit and the result of bringing together this amazing group of high level professionals. It is with great pleasure that I present their combined work. I only hope that you learn as much from reading it as I did from putting it together.

To your success,

Adam Torres

P.S. Let's Connect:
MyInvestmentsMatter.com
Podcast: Money Matters Top Tips with Adam Torres
Instagram: AskAdamTorres
Twitter: @AskAdamTorres

INTRODUCTION

By **LUIS GUAJARDO**

I am a Michigan native and a graduate of the University of Michigan. I began my 10-year career the same year Airbnb was born and have become an expert in the vacation rental industry, with extensive experience in online marketing and web design. I launched my company, Prive Luxury Rentals, in 2012 with only my younger brother, John Donikian, a recent college graduate, and the $5,000 we had to invest in bringing a programmer on board to build our online reservation system.

The vacation rental industry has rapidly evolved. For several years, I researched and field-tested new business models that better fit the changes in the vacation rental space. This proved to be a crash course into the real estate industry, allowing me to bridge the gap and combine my vacation rental knowledge and apply it to real estate investment.

Six years later, I have built my own personal empire of properties in Los Angeles, San Diego, Playa del Carmen, and Tulum—all of which are the base upon which Prive Luxury Rentals grows, doing business for the Coachella Valley Music and Arts Festival near Palm Springs and internationally in Brazil, the Caribbean Islands, and Europe.

Thank you,
Luis Guajardo

CHAPTER 1

BLUEPRINT TO FINANCIAL SUCCESS

By **ADAM TORRES**

Building a house must be done in a specific order. If the walls aren't built, you can't put on the roof. If the foundation is not poured, well, the walls can't be put up. And when do you order the plumbing and electricity? This is an extreme oversimplification of the process of building a home, but you get the point. Follow the rules in established order, or your house will not come out as you intended—or it may simply collapse. The same holds true for investing and planning your financial future. If you don't know and follow the rules, your financial future is subject to collapse, just like a home that's built without the proper foundation or reinforcements.

The rules of investing in real estate (or any investment, for that matter) are fairly simple. But don't confuse "simple" for "easy." They are simple from the standpoint that anyone can execute a well-developed plan with a certain amount of success and certainty. What many people fail to realize is that in developing a plan, you need a team. Throughout this book, you will hear from various professionals that represent the types of team members you will want to recruit and learn from. After you have done your due diligence and assembled your team, what's the first step to success? Many would say you need to find the right investments. Wrong! Instead you need to find the right financial plan.

Creating a financial plan is an art. When plans are customized properly, no two are exactly alike. They often vary in complexity and scope depending on the situation. For example, if you are just graduating from college, you might not have as much complexity to the investing side of your plan. If you accumulated debt along the way, the liability side of your plan may need more attention. Your plan may be geared toward protection and insurance if you are just beginning a family. If you are nearing or in retirement, your plan is likely much more robust. It may even contain multi-generational planning including your grandchildren or great-grandchildren.

All financial plans can benefit from having a few key elements. These elements are not mandatory, but with each addition you increase the clarity of your financial vision of the future.

To begin, you must become clear on your goals and objectives. When I am interviewing a potential client, this is one of the first hurdles to tackle. Many have never really considered exactly how they would like their future financial situation to unfold. To simply state, "I want enough money to retire comfortably" is not a proper way to set a goal. Define "comfortably." Does this mean you would like to play golf daily and travel the world? That is a more expensive retirement than, say, spending your time in the countryside writing novels. The point here is that even though your goals and objectives will change as you progress through life, they should still be tracked and planned for properly.

After you have settled on a starting point for your goals, next it's time to turn your attention to your silent business partner, Uncle Sam. Yes, whether you like it or not, taxes are a reality that must be planned for beyond an annual visit to your tax preparer. Many people think that tax planning is a once-a-year event. The sad truth is that due to the complexity of the tax code, year-round tax planning is essential. Often investors do not maximize their tax savings opportunities because they don't make the time to implement a plan. One of the most common neglected tax planning strategies that many miss out on is contributing to their employer's 401(k) or similar retirement plan. Even worse, many business owners fail to set up a retirement plan for themselves, even when doing so could provide a tax benefit that far outweighs the cost. Every person's situation is unique, but if you are not contributing to a retirement plan, you should reconsider.

How do you know if you are getting wealthier? Create a balance sheet. A balance sheet simply weighs your assets versus liabilities. Why is it important to know whether you are getting richer or poorer? If you track your balance sheet for long enough, you will begin to see trends and will be able to make better informed decisions.

Many people make the same decisions—sometimes incorrectly—about taking on debt or pursuing investments that may not serve their needs simply because they don't know the direction of their overall financial picture and whether they are on track to meet their goals. A balance sheet makes everything clearer.

Equally important to your balance sheet is a cash flow statement. Think of cash flow like oxygen. Without it, you're dead. Cash flow is simply the amount of money that is left over after paying all your expenses, including investment expenses. This is an oversimplification, but you can think of it as the amount of money you have left over at the end of the month. Many times, great plans are derailed because cash flow dries up. If you are in a two-income household and one person loses their job, what does your cash flow look like? Do you have an emergency fund planned? What if an emergency occurs that eats away at your monthly income? Are you prepared? When someone doesn't consider cash flow in their overall financial planning, they are often left off guard when an emergency takes place.

Your insurance coverage is fundamental to your financial planning. Insurance is covered in-depth later in the book, so I will just say that, in my experience, insurance is one of the most important pillars to a successful financial plan. Without adequate insurance coverage for your home, life, and business, you are essentially gambling on the fact that everything will work out fine. Don't gamble with your future. Meet with an insurance professional at least once a year.

Investment planning is the first thing people typically think about when they hear the words "financial plan." It's logical, because investments get much of the attention in media and popular culture. You rarely hear someone on the news say: Have you examined your cash flow lately? Or are you taking on more debt than you can handle? But you will hear news anchors giving you the play-by-play on what took place in the stock market on a day-to-day basis. Or how "earnings season" is playing out and how it will impact the economy. Let's not forget the constant entertainment that the Federal Reserve System provides on whether or not interest rates will rise. Do I think investment planning is necessary? Absolutely. But don't mistake investment planning for timing the market. Timing the market consists of jumping in and out of investments in an attempt to "beat" the market. Instead of timing the market, focus efforts on creating the correct balance between risk and reward for your individual situation. This is done by choosing a group of investments that match your own distinct investment allocation.

Retirement planning has taken on a bad name lately. Many people dread the thought of retirement planning because they can't see themselves retiring. The majority of my clients are business owners. Many of them love what they do and may slow down their involvement in the day-to-day operations of their businesses at some point, but they will likely never retire completely. Advancements in technology have made it so that even so-called "retired" individuals continue consulting after leaving their corporate jobs. Retirement planning is not a question of stopping productivity. Instead, retirement planning should take on a hopeful spirit of choosing what new adventure awaits, and whether or not your current financial planning efforts accommodate your wishes. If you are falling short, what changes need to be made?

Estate planning can be one of the best investments a person can make. Think of estate planning as paying a small fee now to prevent the inevitable future. What is inevitable? Probate. (Keep in mind, I am not a lawyer, so consult one and do not consider this legal advice.) Probate is simply the court charging you to distribute your assets to your heirs by whatever the law in your state deems correct. It's expensive and it is often slow. Why have your estate go through probate if you don't have to? Who wants to pay more in legal fees than needed? Planning on the front end is cheap; going through probate is not.

The second reason to have an estate plan is to keep families together. Yes, I have seen families fall apart due to estate planning issues. Siblings stop talking to each other. Grandkids stop talking to parents. Lawsuits ensue, and courts and lawyers rack up their fees. And why? Because Mom and Dad or Grandpa and Grandma did not have a proper estate plan in place. If you are reading this thinking, "That can never happen to me; my kids would never do that," or, "not in my family," I'm here to tell you that it happens all the time. In my role as a financial planner, I've witnessed this happen more times than I'd like to admit. Estate issues can get complex. Write an estate plan and have control of what happens to the distribution of the assets you spent a lifetime acquiring.

I've given you some of the building blocks of a great financial plan. I'll add one last brick to the wall, specifically for business owners. Succession planning needs to be completed at every stage of your business. Succession planning does not just mean talking about what would happen "if"—it means putting it in writing. Often, when I interview a business owner as a prospective client, I ask them if they have a succession plan in place. A common answer is, "Yes, my kids will take over the business." My response is always the same: "Do they know that?" Many business owners assume—or hope—that their children want to take over the family business, but they can be incorrect in their assumptions. If they do want to take over, that's great, but the owner needs to make sure that the children are involved in the business while he or she is still in the picture. If you're a business owner and your children do not want to continue the business, make sure you have a good "buy sell agreement" or some other vehicle that makes transferring the business simple. You want to avoid a fire sale where the business is sold at a discount because its disposition was not properly planned for. This is an oversimplification of what succession planning entails, but if you have not completed this exercise, put it on the top of your to-do list. Don't wait.

Financial planning gets much more complex the further you get into the process. But don't let that deter you from starting. Just start. Consult an advisor. If you don't have one feel free to reach out to my team at MyInvestmentsMatter.com to schedule a complimentary assessment. Remember, financial plans do not have an end point, so you have nothing to lose by beginning the process. Just as your life changes, your plan should change to suit your needs as those needs develop and shift. As you embark on the planning process, make sure you assemble the right team of professionals to guide you along the way. Don't Google your future success. Just like the builder who assembles a team of professionals to build a beautiful custom home, you must do the same. Assemble seasoned professionals to build a solid financial plan that you can count on.

CHAPTER 2

INVESTING IN RESIDENTIAL ARCHITECTURE:
An Architect's Perspective

By **ANDREW SUZUKI**

Growing up in Los Angeles, I was always interested in how the city was defined by insular and distinctive neighborhoods, defined by economics and all the factors that can be attributed to the economic growth of specific regions. Each neighborhood had a distinct character, each had a history, each had a feel that was unique to its location.

I lived next door to a prominent local architect and was about 8 years old when my father pointed out the buildings, in downtown Los Angeles, that my neighbor had designed. I was impressed that one person could take credit for a huge building, not understanding the complex team of professionals it took to complete such a project.

I played varsity football at a local high school, where the importance of playing with a team was reinforced daily. Everyone had a job to do and if we all did it well, good things happened. We supported each other to the betterment of the team.

I wanted to expand my horizons beyond Southern California and was fortunate enough to be accepted into the University of California at Berkeley. Upon graduation, I entered the Master's program in architecture at UCLA but soon found that I had outgrown my interest in academics and wanted to get on with my life.

I went to work for a residential architect in Orange County designing homes in master planned communities all over the country and world, but focusing on clients in Southern California. I later became Director of Design and/or partner in five firms before founding Suzuki Designs in 2007. We design custom homes, single family and multi-family projects for builders and developers, as well as the occasional remodel. We also provide planning studies to determine the highest and best use for a particular parcel of land in which a client is interested.

Before conscientious architects involve themselves in a project, they should ask their client about their goals. Are they building a property to sell and if so, in the long or short term? Are they building a portfolio of investment properties? Candid answers will drive the hundreds of design decisions the architect will make over the course of design and construction.

Without clear context, designs are useless and fail to illustrate a strategy for success. The investor must define project goals and assemble a team to best provide the advice necessary to achieve those goals. The architect is in a distinct position of being able to offer thoughtful advice, thus enabling the investor to evaluate confusing and sometimes conflicting information.

The single most important decision the investor makes is setting the goal for a particular project or group of projects, as it will inform every subsequent decision. Is the goal to maximize a quick Return on Investment (ROI)? Is the ROI flexible depending on the opportunity, or is the investor willing to take a longer view and maximize their ROI over several years?

The answer will define the type of project(s) they pursue. Rezoning, mapping, and flipping land has traditionally been a great way to grow wealth, but it takes more initial capital and patience to withstand the many obstacles (often known as NIMBYS or Not in My Backyard) thrown at developers in our country. The rewards are potentially great, but don't happen overnight. It takes great political and economic expertise to navigate the labyrinth of challenges that any project will present–remember, if a parcel doesn't have problems, it wouldn't be available. Don't think you've discovered a great secret piece of dirt that has been passed over by the development community. Believe me, you haven't.

If the risks in long-term investing are too daunting, investing in fixer upper or tear down properties usually takes less initial capital and is generally a more manageable endeavor for an investor who is new to real estate. It still takes discipline, good judgement, and patience, but the rewards are commensurate with the risk. Both require the same skills, just in different measures.

For the sake of this chapter, let's assume that you've decided to find a project that can be pursued without a zone change and exists either as a fixer upper or tear down. How do you evaluate its potential? Your team should include a realtor–ask them about their perceptions of the local market. What are the neighborhood socio-economic trends? What are the comparable properties in the immediate neighborhood selling for? What is the market's perception of the neighborhood? Combine the realtor's expertise with your own good judgement about the market potential for this project.

Part of this analysis is defining the probable market segments to whom this home will appeal. Is it a young family with children under 5 years old? A growing family with children under 15? A mature family with school age children (including college age kids)? What about an empty nester couple, or a retired couple? You may ask yourself, "Why define it? Why not design for the widest possible market rather than target a slice of the potential market pool?"

My builder clients say that if they can define one or two market segments as their target markets, they will generally see 50 percent of their sales from within those markets with the other 50 percent coming from segments they never thought would be significant. In other words, they've narrowed their uncertainty by 50 percent. Remember the project I discussed earlier? It took the "universal appeal" approach and missed their market by 90%. Minimizing risk is essential in prudent development. If you can reduce the risk in any category by half, do it.

This next suggestion may seem obvious, but assemble your team for a kick-off meeting. Those meetings have led to our most successful projects. We all get to meet our co-consultants and the owner gets to present their vision. One team, one vision, one goal: No stars, just team players: No divas, just professionals confident in their own expertise and that of their teammates. In the best teams, everyone both understands and respects their lane, but is also confident enough to offer constructive suggestions about larger issues without fear of proprietary jealousy or embarrassment.

Wealth managers, attorneys, contractors, realtors, architects, landscape architects, and planners are all potential sources of pertinent and valuable information—don't be afraid to reach out to them to utilize their talents. I've had landscape architects, interior designers and other real estate professionals offer great design input—we welcome their expertise because we are focused on the goal of the best design possible, regardless of its origin.

Once the team is in place, the context is defined, and the goals are established, the architect can finally start staring at a blank piece of paper and begin synthesizing all the input offered by the investor and co-consultants. The architect mentally, if not figuratively, assembles an opportunities and constraints graphic to further define the design parameters and to plot the way forward.

Don't forget your budget and schedule. Design parameters that are often overlooked include providing the architectural analysis, schematic design, and construction documents on budget and on schedule. What is the construction budget? If the architect isn't constantly aware of the budget and designs a solution that is 20 percent too costly to build, the investor's margin disappears quickly and everyone has just wasted a lot of time and money. Is the home appropriate for its neighborhood and the market segment(s) for which it is intended? If you are in a discretionary market area—that is, a market that can afford a bit higher price than what the investor originally penciled in—then *great*. Raise the price to cover the added expense and hold your breath. But it's far better to design a product that is on budget; if the market surges, adjust the price to take advantage of the upswing and increase your ROI, not merely to cover for your previous mistakes.

Regardless of what part of the country you are pursuing projects in, you must understand and appreciate the impact of ethnic market preferences. If you are focused on California, understanding Feng Shui is important because Asian buyers make up a large portion of the market. Deny the reality of Feng Shui to Asians and you risk alienating a large pool of potential buyers. For example, consider: How the home is placed on the lot? Is the entry orientation relative to the lot and neighborhood correct? Are the room placements, stair location, view corridors all in compliance with Feng Shui guidelines? The investor doesn't have to believe in Feng Shui, but must believe that their market believes in it.

My Indian clients regularly have large family gatherings to share meals, visit, and watch their children entertain the family. A small stage or place where a child can perform is a subtle but welcome design feature—a raised stair landing works well, but we've also designed small raised decks or balconies in rear yards to serve as impromptu stages. No matter where you are, appreciation and awareness of cultural sensitivities is essential in designing a successful residential project.

While California has traditionally led the nation in residential design trends, neighboring states have been quick to adapt them to their region and to their respective market's preferences. Open floor plans, long a design staple of the informal California lifestyle, have made their way into the consciousness of the rest of the country through home improvement television and movies. Casual outdoor seating, entertainment centers with fire pits, wet bars, and lounging areas are all in high demand.

Be aware that most, if not all, jurisdictions now have formal design review boards that act as an adjunct to the planning commission. These design review boards review the planning and design aspects of any project under their jurisdiction and they can be very subjective. They can impose costly design features or ask for additional design exhibits that, to the uninitiated, may seem arbitrary and overblown. True enough, these additional requirements may be onerous, but you must get approval before moving on to the permitting process. You can fight them, but it's always better to negotiate because the investor has little or no leverage. The architect should research the jurisdictional design review protocol and inform the investor team of any potential future impediments to a swift approval.

Designing homes in Southern California is a study in understanding subtle but distinct local preferences. What works on the Westside may not work in Pasadena. What works in Newport Beach may not be appropriate for Montecito—but then again, it might. This is where the experienced residential architect's experience becomes invaluable.

If you're investing out-of-state, the same protocols for designing for California are still in play, but you must adjust them for regional idiosyncrasies and preferences. The architect designing a custom home has the advantage of asking their clients directly about their preferences. If you're building to sell, you must design for probable market segments but the product must stay flexible enough to accommodate outlier or unanticipated segments.

What the investor must never do is to design for their own tastes or preferences. Unless you or your peers are going to buy what you build, this is the cardinal sin of investors. You are clearly successful in your chosen field or you wouldn't be researching investment opportunities—but your expertise is not necessarily transferable to market segment identification, economic analysis, or design. Trust your team. Trust your instincts about the team members themselves. Contribute your ideas but be open to expert advice that might be counterintuitive. Learn from your mistakes, as well as the mistakes of those you hire. Your ability to read people and your B.S. meter are your best assets in guiding your team and making decisions.

Remember, unless you are building a custom home for you and your family, you are building a product. Define it. Design it. Nurture it. Know you are going to ultimately sell it and move on to the next project. Don't fall in love with it!

CHAPTER 3

ENGINEERS AND REAL ESTATE DEVELOPMENTS

By **CELESTIN HARITON**

Why bring an engineer into a real estate deal when you can often use a contractor to do seemingly the same job? Engineers can add a great amount of value to a project from many perspectives. Contractors are often very good at building and provisioning materials for a structure, or fixing the systems within, but they are not always knowledgeable about the best design methods and current legislative requirements that will ultimately save the client money. Professional engineers are a strategic partner with building developers, owners, and architects to identify systems that are most cost effective, compliant with regulations, help realize long term utility costs, and provide prestige to a project.

Now, I am not talking about any type of engineer. I am talking about consulting engineers related to the construction industry. The main engineering fields that are related to this industry are civil, structural, mechanical, plumbing, and electrical. Engineers are also experts at evaluating the systems of an existing building and can advise the potential buyer regarding the condition and viability of existing systems. This is beneficial in determining maintenance issues that are urgent or that can be deferred.

What do civil engineers do?

They ensure that the site of a real estate development, from the smallest home to the largest campus, is adequately prepared to receive above–and below–ground development. Civil engineers ensure buildings do not get flooded by generating adequate soil slope that drains rainwater away from the site. Below surface drainage is also considered and the system of pipes are sized correctly with proper material selection. They also plan and coordinate locations for incoming utilities entering the building such as water, gas, and electricity to ensure that they serve the needs of the development. One of the biggest responsibilities for a civil engineer is to provide a drainage system where sewage waste is removed accordingly from the site into nearby designated municipal connections.

What do structural engineers do?

In short, they make sure that buildings can hold themselves up as well as stand up to natural elements. It is a vital requirement, not to mention morbid, that a building allow all tenants enough time to evacuate safely prior to eminent collapse. Structural engineers consider the vagaries of nature, from earthquakes to hurricanes, even extreme rain. They work with owners and architects to select the most adequate and cost effective structural system for the program of real estate development. Structural engineers make provisions within their design to allow for openings of elevators, stairs, skylights, windows, doors, and utilities. They also incorporate additional support of heavy equipment within the building. Structural engineers account for design elements that seem impossible to accomplish. Think about how a skyscraper can look as if it is made entirely from glass, standing up so elegantly against the skyline. This is one example of the structural engineer's accomplishment: building taller buildings with minimal material without compromising the safety of the structure–seemingly defying gravity.

What do mechanical engineers do?

A modern indoor space would likely be very uncomfortable to live or work in without provisions for air conditioning and heating. Mechanical engineers are adept at designing systems that are cost effective and tailored to a customer's specific needs. Sometimes the savings inherent in choosing the correct system are realized immediately, other times during the lifetime of the building. Mechanical engineers work with their team to design the real estate to be the most energy efficient possible, with an eye on energy savings regulations, as mandated by more and more states. Ultimately, mechanical engineers design systems so that the comfort of heating and cooling are felt without excessive noise, drafts, or uneven climate conditioning of a space. They also ensure that the air distribution system is "balanced" in the entire building, so no one part of a project is cooler or warmer than other parts.

What do plumbing engineers do?

Plumbing engineers bring water in and out of a building efficiently. Working with a plumbing engineer can ensure that water is delivered efficiently and at the right pressure to avoid spending extra money on oversized systems. They are also adept at removing waste from within the building quietly and without disruption to the occupants. Current building codes include water saving requirements that plumbing engineers are very familiar with and can easily implement. They are also responsible for designing any gas connections that the tenants may require in a building.

What do electrical engineers do?

It would seem obvious that an electrical engineer brings electricity into the building and he or she certainly does that. What an electrical engineer does best, however, is size systems to make the most efficient installation. On a construction project, energy savings and safety of systems are the electrical engineer's primary focus. For example, specifying lighting systems such as LED can realize significant savings for the owner or developer. It is the electrical engineer's responsibility to implement state programs mandating energy savings, including compliance to Title 24. Electrical engineers also provide lighting studies and advise the architect on the optimal location of light fixtures and power services.

This is merely a summary of general services that can be implemented across the various trades by the consulting engineers in a construction project. These valuable features should be incorporated as part of a larger dialogue to be conducted with the developer, owner, and architect of a property. While sometimes costly at the onset of a project, the cost savings of implementing a professional team will be realized over time and add to the prestige of the project.

Sustainability

Sustainability is defined as the avoidance of the depletion of natural resources to maintain an ecological balance. Man's relationship with the environment has always been complicated by the tension between man's desire to alter the environment he lives in to better serve his needs and his desire to preserve natural resources for prolonged use. Sustainability has been understood and practiced by civilizations to various levels of success throughout human history.

Modern society's concern with sustainability is focused on longevity and reusability of resources, as well as creating reusable sources of energy. While this approach is applicable in many areas of development, it has tremendous efficacy in the construction and real estate industries. Many examples can be seen where the value of a property can be enhanced and made more marketable by incorporating sustainability features in the design, either as part of a new construction or during the remodeling process of an existing structure. How is sustainability accomplished across these different fields of consulting engineering in construction?

Civil Engineering

Choosing an appropriate site and providing efficient drainage features are examples of civil engineering's contribution to sustainability. Other examples of sustainable features that he or she implement often may include reuse and remediation of brownfields.

This takes a previously undesirable and "unbuildable" land parcel and provides it a new life. Water filtering drainage features such as bio-swales are also extremely common and popular these days. Bio-swales can also be implemented on existing sites and have the added benefit of beautifying the real estate development. Creating a pond is another example of a feature that both adds beauty and serves to retain water for irrigation purposes and infiltration into ground aquifers.

Structural Engineering

Structural engineers are the stewards of sustainability whereby they can help dictate the geometry and materials of a building, thus improving the use of resources and construction methods to avoid waste. Locally produced bricks can be one example. Lumber is another example. Properly sourced wood from sustainable forests is considered a renewable material. Forests in this way serve as a carbon sink as trees absorb carbon dioxide from the atmosphere while they grow. Structural engineers also work to incorporate sustainability features such as "green" roof gardens, solar panels, and daylighting (skylights, large window openings, etc.) into the support system of any real estate development project.

Mechanical Engineering

In addition to using efficient heating, ventilation, and air conditioning (HVAC) equipment, mechanical engineers are also adept at modeling the energy consumption of a building and working with architects to implement energy saving features into the shell of the building. For example, they can make recommendations regarding the insulation level to be built into the walls and roof of the building which complies with energy codes and help the thermal performance of the entire real estate development. Mechanical engineers also recommend the proper type of glass that works with the shell of a building to reduce energy consumption. They can design sophisticated sensors and control panels into a room where the air conditioning can automatically self-adjust when the tenants are away. Mechanical engineers can also help with introducing natural heating and ventilation elements into a building.

Plumbing Engineering

Water is a major source of life. One can survive longer solely on water than on food alone. It is necessary for the maintenance of life and many of humanity's processes. While seemingly available in copious quantities across the globe in oceans and ice, the water available for human consumption is surprisingly quite limited. It is the preservation of this precious resource where the plumbing engineer is most valuable. Plumbing engineers can implement water-saving features such as low-flow devices within a building, rain capturing devices for water to be used for irrigation and reusing wastewater in the building for other purposes, like using wastewater from sinks to flush toilets.

Electrical Engineering

There are many options for reducing electricity use within a building. Using energy efficient LED lighting and incorporating occupancy sensors are two major ways energy can be saved. LED lighting is much more efficient than fluorescent lighting (not to mention incandescent lighting) and can provide a varied range of color hues that can serve to improve the appearance of a space. It also provides options for controllability that could only be achieved with great effort using other lighting methods. Occupancy sensors and controls are another way to conserve energy. They can include timers that ensure lights are not kept on beyond the required time of use. Occupant sensing controls can also act as motion sensors that turn lights off the after a space is vacated. Another popular power saving feature is the use of solar panels. Electrical engineers can advise the real estate development team on the proper size and quantity of photovoltaic cells.

While we certainly have the freedom to conduct our lives in the manner that we choose and pursue the endeavors that best serve our needs, we also have a social and moral responsibility to preserve the environment both for our use and for the survival and enjoyment of those who come after us. The better we take care of our planet and our environment now, the better they will take care of us in future generations.

CHAPTER 4

HOW TO BRAND AND MARKET YOURSELF IN REAL ESTATE

By **CHIRAG SAGAR**

Marketing has been around for two millennia, since vendors started chiseling their goods, spices, and tools on rocks. The printing press expanded opportunities for marketing with brochures and flyers; billboards changed the landscape, as did the radio, TV and, eventually, the Internet.

The purpose of marketing is to attract attention, create interest, and initiate someone to purchase a product or service. In order to take advantage of marketing, you need to establish your branding and positioning.

There are basic fundamentals to keep in mind when building a product and brand. Growing your brand creates professional opportunities, allows you to get a better job, more clients for your company, industry recognition, and builds you up to become a credible thought leader.

Personal Brand vs. Business Brand:

One thing worth noting is the stark difference in strategy between building a personal brand and building a brand for your business. It's common to see businesses with mission and vision statements; in real estate, these statements can be even more direct. Google how the biggest industry leaders in your particular niche describe themselves.

If you look at James Lang LaSalle (JLL), they are a fortune 500 company that has the following mission statement: *provide commercial real estate services for organizations of all sizes, across industries, and all over the world. Whether you're looking for space solutions for your business, or for help making or managing an investment, we've got a team to deliver.* Their mission is clearly defined. Each decision they make is directed towards accomplishing their mission.

Similarly, a personal brand can be defined by your long-term vision on what you want to accomplish in your life. Once you establish your vision statement for yourself and your business, ask yourself the following question: *"Will the following activity or decision bring me one step closer to accomplishing my mission and vision?"* If the answer is "no," then that's how you decide not to take on that meeting, try that new marketing approach, or join that advisory board. It allows you to say "no" so that you can focus on the decisions that will bring you one step closer to accomplishing your vision and mission.

Ultimately, your personal brand and business brand will separate you from all the others. It's the emotional connection back to who you are and your company's DNA. It's what makes you unique.

Beyond establishing your mission and vision, you'll need to define your and your company's values. Personal and business values can be family, friends, or community. Values are one of the key indicators in choosing the right business partners, hiring the best staff to grow your company, and working with clients who share similar traits and characteristics. This isn't always the case, but knowing your values will get you one step closer to fostering your community of like-minded kin.

Your marketing tactics are going to depend on the overall strategy of your personal and business brand. As you hone in on your strategy, try to answer the following questions:

1. What is your overall business?

2. What is your mission statement? Your vision statement?

3. What are your core values?

4. How do you want to be perceived?
   What do you want to be known for?

5. Where do you want to be in the next year?
   3 years? 5 years? 10 years? 20 years?

6. What are you offering?

7. What are your services?

8. What makes you or your business unique?

If you're able to answer all of these questions in a concise, concrete, specific, measurable, and time-bound way, you'll be able to understand your overall purpose and goals you'd like to achieve. You'll have better direction in designing your website, know which social media platforms make the most sense for you to build your presence, what keywords to rank in implementing your SEO strategy, and what other marketing channels you should be using.

Depending on how you want to position yourself online, it might be effective to build a personal brand as well as a business brand. It's nearly double the amount of work. You'll need to assess your financial situation and consider if you want to hire outside support to help build both personal and business brands. Consistency is the greatest factor in building your digital presence.

Building your digital brand is similar to being in great physical shape. You need to work out consistently, eat healthy, rest, drink water, and take nutrients, minerals, and vitamins. In some cases, you might need a personal trainer to hold you accountable, show you how to properly exercise, what foods to eat to get in shape. But unlike physical fitness, which requires you to do the work, you can hire someone else to assist you in your marketing efforts to do the work for you. With your guidance they will help you achieve your personal and business marketing goals.

Building the brand of Destination Luxury took hours every day: writing content, producing high-end videos, coordinating events, and orchestrating all marketing channels to achieve our results. You can do the bare minimum needed to get your brand going, but remember that it'll take time every day to build a brand.

Once you've established your marketing and business goals and when you know how you want to be positioned, here's a short checklist of measures you can take to establish your brand:

- **Get professional photos.** Use them on all of your digital marketing channels. As you'll see in the front cover of this book, follow the author's examples. If you have the money to afford it, hire a professional to take your headshot.

- **Build a professional website.** This is where you can brand yourself at your discretion. It creates an important level of consistency and establishes your brand.

- **Pay attention to your email signature.** This is often overlooked. Include your photo or company logo, your name, title, company name, phone number, address, website, email, and social media links.

- **Create a professional brand video.** It will highlight who you are, what you do, where you're going, and how you can help others.

- **Establish your social media pages.** Secure the following social media accounts: Facebook, LinkedIn, Instagram, Twitter, YouTube, and personal blog using your company name or personal name. Use the same ID and handles for all the platforms. (I.e. for Destination Luxury – you can find us on all social media platforms by typing in **@Destinationluxury** or finding us on Facebook at **www.facebook.com/destinationluxury**, Instagram at **www.Instagram.com/destinationluxury**, etc.)

Marketing Channels

With so many marketing channels to select from, I've narrowed the scope on which ones will make the most sense for real estate businesses. Each one serves its own purpose and not all of them will be the best fit for you. I'll break down the function and purpose of each and provide a real estate-related example and an individual that uses the platform well. You'll have a basic understanding of what to do on each platform and which one could be the best fit for you.

Website

When it comes to establishing an online presence, a website is your digital home base. It's the online hub where anyone can go to learn more about who you are, where to find you online, what you do, services you offer, and become familiar with your brand. As technology has advanced, there are many tools and platforms that allow you to easily build a website with a sleek and modern look. Having a website allows for complete creative control, design, and brand alignment. Unlike most social media pages, you're not restricted to their design. On your website, your imagination can be your reality. If you need some inspiration, there are many ready-made website platforms that provide you with the structure you need.

Even if you're working for a large firm where you're restricted on the type of content you promote, you can still purchase your website domain name and emphasize that your thoughts are your own. Purchase your name from a website hosting company like GoDaddy. My website is **chiragsagar.com**; I separate my personal brand from Destination Luxury. Showcase who you are on the website by including your purpose, vision, mission, and brand positioning statement. Consider your website your most prized digital real estate. All your marketing channels will serve as bridges connecting people to your website.

There are many website building tools that are free, and ones where you might need to pay a nominal fee to build your brand. Wordpress, Wix, Weebly, Strikingly, or SquareSpace are all great options and offer easily customizable websites. If you want to build a brand but don't have the time or want to build something more robust, you can hire a company to build out a customized website.

Keep the content on the website as direct and simple as possible. Remember the acronym, KISS (Keep It Simple, Stupid). Use professional photos and keep your design as modern and clean as possible. Examples of great websites are **www.dljlawfirm.com**, **www.kermanillp.com**, and **www.barbaracorcoran.com**.

Blog

Blogs are one of the best ways to drive traffic to your website. This is where you can publish long-form content to share your expertise in real estate and demonstrate the value that you provide. The question is: How do you know what type of content to create? How do you write long-form content that can be valuable to your readers?

Check out Answer the Public (**www.answerthepublic.com**) for the most searched phrases and questions in regards to real estate. Based on the most commonly asked questions in your specific field, create content based on the most searched keywords. The goal is to write articles that are more than 500 words long so that the content can be crawled or recognized by Google. As you become more comfortable, it'll become easy to write content beyond 1,000 words, which is the type of content we've seen generating the most buzz on Google and social media. Examples of great real estate blogs are **www.redfin.com**, **www.gavingrantrealtor.com/blog**, and **www.manausa.com/blog**.

Emails

The most surefire way to communicate with potential clients is by capturing their email address. This is how you can upsell, resell, hire staff, and deliver engaging content.

Using tools like MailChimp, Constant Contact, or Hubspot, you'll be able to send mass emails to your following with a few easy clicks. There is a slight learning curve in setting up these emails, but if you follow through, you'll have a consistent way to share your content, offerings, events, open houses, and additional information with your loyal followers. Maintaining consistency is the key to develop rapport with potential clients.

If you have new homes for sale, product offerings, or stories you want to share, this is the means by which you can share it. This will let you track the number of opens, clicks, conversions, and sales you've received.

Customer Relationship Management (CRM) System

If you have thousands of connections, you need software that will track each time you connect with one of your contacts. You can easily track when you last emailed someone, spoke to them on the phone, and recorded what your last encounter was with all of your connections.

There are countless tools like Zoho, Salesforce IQ, Pipedrive, Hubspot CRM, Monday.com CRM, and many more. They all work well, but it comes down to which one suits you the best. Track your conversation and touch points with all of your contacts.

Facebook

With a third of Earth's population using Facebook, it's the one platform that cannot be ignored. It's the best way to establish your brand and convert leads back to your website. The first step is to setup and build a Facebook page, if you already haven't. Similar to your website, keeping your branding consistent is how you will establish your credibility. You can change the URL of your professional Facebook page to match your website. My company's website is **www.destinationluxury.com** and the Facebook URL is **www.facebook.com/destinationluxury**. Apply this to all of your social media accounts. Use professional headshots and keep your profile photos consistent across all social media platforms.

Shark Tank's very own real estate mogul, Barbara Corcoran, does a remarkable job of maintaining brand integrity and creating motivational, real estate-focused content on her Facebook page: **www.facebook.com/TheBarbaraCorcoran.** As you can see, she's elevated her Facebook presence and creates strong engaging content on social media.

Remember, capturing emails is still the best way to communicate with clients. Unless you're spending money on Facebook, it's difficult to build a brand organically without spending advertising money to boost your posts. In addition to YouTube and now LinkedIn, video content is very valuable to Facebook and is great way to build your brand. If you have the budget, you can spend, at minimum, several dollars per day to geo-target your audience. You can pinpoint them by zip code, income level, age range, family, net worth, interests, and more. The customer acquisition cost—amount you need to spend in order to get a new client—will only increase. Facebook has been charging more money on their platform and it continuously increases.

This requires creating Facebook content and ads that will get your audience's attention. The best ads are designed to look like they are part of your feed—like they are not an ad at all.

YouTube

As described in the last section, Facebook's biggest video competitor is YouTube. Here's the beauty of creating video content— it's reusable and it can be recycled and repurposed for all video-related mediums (Facebook, LinkedIn, YouTube, and Instagram).

As a realtor it's always a homerun to take video content of a beautiful home, especially luxury properties. One of our viral videos on Destination Luxury was an interview with the builder of a $26-million-dollar home in Malibu (See it here: **www.youtube.com/ watch?v=t_C-QAUuR-I.** *More than 300,000 views*).

What if you're not a realtor? What happens if you're in insurance or selling mortgages? What type of content performs well here? Interestingly, you can still create valuable content by using one of your long form articles and summarizing your key points in the form of a video. You can reference Answer the Public to find commonly asked questions on Google. Here is an example of a video that performed very well on YouTube: **www.youtube.com/ watch?v=IxyDtG6Mw04** (more than 12,000 views).

Videos that perform well include those with insights, motivational content, FAQ or Q&As, informative content, or beautiful scenery. You can replicate what YouTube influencers with a large following are doing.

Instagram

In June 2018, there were more than 1 billion active monthly users on Instagram. It's one of the most powerful and growing platforms suitable for professionals and businesses to develop a following. As with other social media platforms, begin by establishing your brand on Instagram, using your professional photo and standard bio to maintain brand consistency. Once completed, identify your target market and use the search feature to source relevant hashtags related to your interests.

Instagram is a visual platform. Quality photos matter. An example of a real estate professional doing an excellent job is luxury realtor, Josh Reef @joshreef. You'll notice that his photos are consistent and focus on high-end real estate. Josh has amassed more than 60,000 Instagram followers and receives a plethora of sales opportunities from his Instagram account.

When posting content, you'll notice that you're able to use up to 30 hashtags. Maximize them. It's how individuals in your niche can find you organically. Find hashtags relevant to the content you're posting, new hashtags relevant to you, and commonly used hashtags to get new followers. A great strategy is the 10/10/10 hashtag strategy.

- 10 smaller hashtags (10,000 - 50,000 total posts)

- 10 mid-size hashtags (50,000 - 200,000 total posts)

- 10 large hashtags (20,000 - 2,000,000 total posts)

Instagram is a powerful way to engage and start conversations. It's how you can generate new lead flow. Comment and direct message (DM) new leads with relevant content that they care about. Don't spam. How do you feel when you get a telemarketer calling you? Annoyed? Frustrated? If you're like most people, you probably hang up the phone within seconds or ignore the call. So why would you initiate a conversation this way with a stranger online?

Research the person and find a commonality. If you know they're interested in sports, family, cars, or another topic, it's worth sending them an article that they'll care about and read related to their interests. It's the start to establishing rapport and getting a positive response.

Twitter

The main function of Twitter is to serve as a news resource guide and a platform to connect and engage others. It's a strong business development platform. Navigating the search bar for relevant hashtags is how you filter quality contacts and content. Get a Twitter handle (username) that is consistent with the rest of your brand and maintain your consistent bio.

Determine your target audience. If you're focused on sales and finding new clients, create content that's hyper-focused on sales efforts. Sharing articles, links, original articles, and long-form content is a great way to build rapport. Unlike other platforms, Twitter is meant to engage individuals directly, just as you would interact with someone at a networking event. Twitter is the online version of networking where you can join in and add value to a conversation.

When formulating content, follow this Twitter posting strategy:

- 30 percent should be links to your own website

- 30 percent should be talking about business or sharing business-related content

- 40 percent should consist of personal interaction, small talk, commenting, and networking

Sprout Social is a social media management tool created to help businesses find new customers and grow their social media presence. Buffer analyzes and automatically schedules your tweets to post at the best possible time. Luxury realtor @joshreef also does a remarkable job sharing content. With his 40,000 Twitter followers, he's sourcing leads from social media to get new listings and find new buyers. It would be worthwhile to monitor and replicate how he uses his Twitter.

LinkedIn

LinkedIn began as a professional online résumé and has since evolved into a professional content platform. Because LinkedIn is primarily a business-focused social media platform, everyone maintains a professional composure. Keeping your branding consistent, you might also want to highlight your prior work experience in detail here.

Request testimonials from clients and ask them to post them on LinkedIn and Yelp. These references are a great resource, especially for realtors in sales.

Create valuable content, similar to what you post on your blog or Facebook page, that can be great content to publish. Video is becoming more popular on LinkedIn. You can recycle the same content on Facebook and YouTube and publish this same content on LinkedIn.

Find and join real estate LinkedIn groups. Create a group and curate the conversation. This is where you can build your community to refer clients to one another. Start small if you must and add more people to the group as you continue to expand your network.

Here are several LinkedIn real estate groups worth joining: Social media for real estate (**www.linkedin.com/groups/1812050/profile**), Inman Smart about Real Estate group (**www.linkedin.com/groups/59/profile**), and Real Estate Professionals Referral Group (**www.linkedin.com/groups/118487/profile**).

Without the appropriate branding and positioning of your brand, it's difficult to know how to navigate social media. Think of marketing as a jazz ensemble. The instruments are the different social media platforms and the players playing the instruments practice and have a strategy in place. In a similar way, you need to use the social media platforms consistently and need a defined strategy. Like working out and staying in good physical shape, building a brand requires a proper allocation of time. Assess if it's worth bringing in specialists, consultants, or outsourced support to assist you with your marketing needs.

If you have any questions about marketing or branding, I'm more than happy to provide a free assessment. You may contact me directly at Chirag@MoneyMattersTopTips.com.

CHAPTER 5

MORTGAGES MATTER TOO

By **DAVID WESTLEY**

After a restless night of sleep, I awoke at 5:40 a.m. with the sudden realization that the markets were in the middle of a meltdown. This was in early December of 2007; the crisis was likely to affect a large pipeline of loans for my friends and clients that I had worked with for nearly 35 years and in a relatively stable mortgage industry.

Mortgages are loans made on real estate that are secured by the real property. If values declined and loans exceeded the values of the properties, I knew it would create a dangerous situation for the economy. Credit started to collapse right before our very eyes. Some of my best clients had transactions pending and stood to lose their down payments and dream homes. Luckily, I was able to work through most issues with lenders and the banks issuing mortgages because of the strong lenders I worked with and my past experience, which allowed me to foresee these difficulties. I have never sold past clients risky subprime products, always relying on the fundamental soundness of any transaction, so there was never a chance that my clients would be caught up in the turbulent waters ahead.

Credit is a tool that should be used wisely. Lenders have been loaning money for thousands of years and many of the economic downturns throughout history have come from the misuse of extending credit. The mortgage meltdown was no different. Sound principles that have been the hallmark of my career—namely, to determine a borrower's ability to repay a loan—were replaced with a mirror test to see if a borrower could fog the glass. To complicate the dangerous practice, Wall Street repackaged subprime loans and sold them as premium debt packages. It all would have continued just fine if housing prices continued to rise and the few foreclosures could be absorbed by the markets.

A foreclosure occurs when a borrower cannot repay the loan and the lender must take possession of the property to satisfy the loan. The problem with subprime loans is that when borrowers begin to default, and there are fewer buyers than sellers, the prices of properties fall. A correction can be healthy for a market but in this instance, we were headed toward a collapse, lenders began to panic. I began to lose sleep because my clients were looking to me to help them get their deals done. Their futures were in my hands and I needed to deliver.

For years, I have commenced every transaction the same way, by seeking to understand my client's needs and asking them the right questions. What is your income? What are your assets? How much do you want to borrow? What type of loan are you interested in? What is the value of the property you are acquiring? What rate do we need to get to make the deal work? I can then set my sights on getting the best deal once I understand the transaction that is being requested.

So, let's get down to the business of the transaction. The loan is just the paperwork and calculation needed to transfer the money from the lender to the borrower. The loan is the necessary evil, getting us to our objective: the real estate. Getting the right real estate is the foundation of getting the right loan. The biggest purchase most of us will make is our lifetime is the purchase of our home. It is not only our biggest financial investment; it is also an emotional investment that we make to enrich the lives of our family.

With most home loans, the lender is making a larger financial investment in the home than the buyer. The buyer will usually purchase the home by putting 20 percent into the purchase as a down payment. For example, a purchase price of an $800,000 house would have a $160,000 down payment and the loan would be $640,000. The lender will securitize their loan through a quasi-government agency like Fannie Mae or Freddie Mac to make sure you, the buyer, gets the lowest interest rate. Fannie Mae and Freddie Mac are private companies sponsored by the U.S. government to help keep interest rates low for homebuyers. Government-sponsored enterprises (GSEs) are privately owned but receive support from the Federal Government which provides a secondary market for home mortgages from lenders who originate them. Freddie and Fannie have strict guidelines and require that your home conform to them. Your home also must meet all state, county, and city building codes and regulations. The structure must be inhabitable, have a working bathroom and kitchen, measure a certain square footage, have working fire alarms and meet all other guidelines.

Each lender will require an independent third party appraiser to appraise the property to determine its value and make sure all conditions are met and comply with the guidelines mentioned above. An appraiser will inspect the house, take pictures of each room, note any upgrades or deficiencies, and measure each room and the house. The appraiser will note any upgrades and or deficiencies. They will determine the condition of the home, ranging from excellent to poor condition. Through the Real Estate Multiple Listing Services of the area, the appraiser will find homes that have sold or are currently for sale within a very close geographical location and compare the sale prices. Depending on the area, these "comparable" homes will be within a small radius. These comparable homes will be reviewed, driven by, and photographed. Comparisons will note the condition, number of rooms, square footage, amenities, and price. The appraiser compares a minimum of four to six comparable homes near the property that are sold or for sale, giving a greater weight to homes sold within the last six months to determine the fair market value property. Once all the calculations are complete, the appraiser will determine what they calculate the value of the loan to be. An extra bathroom may add $15,000+ or-, a swimming pool may add $25,000.

After the housing crisis mortgages on all properties became more difficult to secure as new laws were passed to protect the consumer. When the dust settled, credit was restored and the number of mortgage brokers that remained in the industry were severely reduced. There are very few that had the chops to weather the 2008 crisis. I survived because my knowledge of the mortgage industry is vast. I also forged many relationships in my career.

More than fifty percent of residential properties are financed through lenders that are backed by Freddie Mac and Fannie Mae. Commercial financing has a greater diversity of lenders, each of which have specific criteria for the types of loans they originate. Banks are one source, but commercial lenders consist of insurance companies, pension funds, hedge funds, CMBS, and REITS etc. Each of these entities are looking for a specific type of transaction.

For example, one of my clients came to me with a six-unit apartment building that needed a $1.2 million loan. I knew that this loan was too small for a large insurance company or for the commercial division of a large, well-known national bank. The loan my client needed was a perfect fit for a community bank that has nine branches in Southern California. We could get terms and an interest rate similar to what the national banks were quoting on larger transactions. This turned out to be a great loan for my client by just knowing the right lender.

Lenders define the value of a commercial property's income, or "capitalization rate," which is based on the income of that property. Net operating income is calculated by adding up all the expenses associated with a property and deducting them from the gross income. For example, my client purchased his apartment building for $1.6 million and he expected it to generate $128,000 in net operating income every year. So, the cap rate on the property was 8 percent. Divide the price by the income.

Cap rates aside, loans on commercial properties can get complicated. Most lenders will grade A, B, C, of the property on the condition of the property. Some lenders will not lend on C. Some will not lend on older buildings; some will not make loans with tucked-under parking, while others will not loan on properties that have inadequate parking. Having seen thousands of transactions in Los Angeles gives me a sense of what property is right for particular lenders. When I come across a property built in the 1920s or 30s, I immediately ask about the parking because I know that many of these buildings have no parking at all and therefore only certain lenders will lend on it.

Knowing that a mortgage lender has his pulse on the lender's guidelines is an important criterion. The kinds of properties lenders want in their portfolios is constantly changing as loan committees or personnel at the lenders change their minds based upon the amount of money the institution wants to lend, the economy, the financial health of the company, economic forecasts, a mix of their loans outstanding, or a wholesale change in the business. But, as a rule, insurance companies generally make loans on larger properties, like major office buildings. Pension funds can lend on large construction projects, and hedge funds are great sources for mezzanine or bridge financing. A lender should know what's in the market.

The financial crisis happened because of faulty, misleading, and dangerous loan products that left the borrower holding the bag.

Interest rates were low, home prices were rising, and everyone could get a loan because buying a home was considered a "sure bet." People were living large by refinancing and taking out loans on their equity. To make borrowing easy, there were easy loan approvals, low teaser beginning rates, negative interest rates, and stated income loans. Lenders offered products that virtually encouraged fraud on loan applications. One man got a loan by writing on his loan application that he was working overtime earning $12,000 a month making French fries at McDonald's. This fact was never verified with a pay stub or tax returns. Fraud was encouraged by banks that sold loans to Wall Street, which then packaged the loans into tranches that were sold to the public.

Lending ground to a virtual halt during the crisis as foreclosures began (how long could Mr. French Fry make his mortgage payments?), defaults rose, and home values plummeted. What happened to my clients? They were not affected by the crisis. As an honest mortgage banker, I never put my clients into a predatory or bad loan. I never allowed them to purchase a home that they could not afford—and I knew what they could afford because I understood their financial situations. Loans that had low payments for six months or a year and then skyrocketed were never an option for my clients—I never put these products on the table. What seems like common sense had gone out the window for many people, but I was raised in a well-off but financially conservative household. Both of my parents lived through the Great Depression of the 1930s. My parents were strict and serious with me and my siblings. My chores had to be done correctly before I received my allowance, which helped me learn the value of a dollar. I was educated at the University of Southern California, where I received my Bachelor's and Master's degrees in finance with an emphasis in real estate, and I pursued continuing education, including receiving a real estate broker's license, California mortgage license, national mortgage license, and doing landscape architecture work at the University of California, Los Angeles. I remain interested in learning about financial planning, appraisal, economics, and psychology, and I read extensively, travel the world, and love to learn about history. All of this contributes to my grounded perspective as a mortgage broker.

When I arrived at the office early on that December morning, I informed the staff that we were "all hands-on deck." We would need to work around the clock to save our clients lower interest rates and their down payments. One client, a famous movie producer, was in the process of getting a jumbo loan of $2.5 million on his $4.25 million dream home. Our lender added additional underwriting requirements at the last minute to stop the loan because of the looming mortgage meltdown. With the down payment and closing costs we were approaching $2 million. The down payment that was in escrow and my client's cash reserves were depleted .The bank wanted more reserves. What seemed impossible to those around me fell into place because of my experience. The solution was in the financial statements—his personal and corporate financials. I convinced the underwriter to allow funds from my client's business to flow into his personal account, using those funds as reserves. Trust me when I say that your average bank loan officer does not have the knowledge and is not in the position to negotiate with a senior underwriter how to effectively mitigate such an impasse. Very few mortgage executives are taught or encouraged to learn how to read sophisticated corporate financial statements or tax returns. The client procured a letter from his CFO that moving this cash would not impact operations. Once this process was complete, the loan was closed.

We worked around the clock to get deals done and navigate our clients through the beginning of the housing crisis. As lenders feared making loans and banks virtually stopped doing almost any business, we would waltz through to lenders we had known for years and get our transactions completed. Those lenders knew that our transactions were fundamentally sound and they helped us take care of our clients.

December of 2007 quickly gave way to early 2008, when the subprime mortgage crisis precipitated a crash in the American Dream of owning a home. Crash, panic, and volatility in the financial markets was a result of the greed of Wall Street and its flawed financial modeling that assumed home prices would always rise. We began to focus on commercial properties with institutional lenders and adjusted to the new, more rigorous forms accompanying the almost frozen credit climate that replaced the freewheeling mirror test lending practices. Through these changes in the industry our business practices have remained the same.

CHAPTER 6

BEST PRACTICES IN ACCOUNTING FOR REAL ESTATE INVESTMENT PROJECTS

By JEFF NEUMEISTER

It was the middle of 2005 and Acme Holdings ("Acme") was scoping out possible sites for its next development project. As a real estate developer and investor, Acme had initiated, managed, and sold dozens of successful mixed-use development projects. This next one was to be comprised of condominiums, a boutique hotel, and retail space mirroring three other projects that were currently underway. While most of these development projects were financed directly by Acme through cash and bank loans, this one was going to be a joint venture with a strategic affiliate, Gekko, Inc. ("Gekko"). Gekko did not share any ownership with Acme but was a referral source for viable sites and was sometimes used as a subcontractor for elements of a project.

Upon execution of the mutually agreed upon operating agreement, Acme and Gekko formed a new LLC to contain the activities of this new development project. A pair of loans totaling $40 million were taken out from two different lenders in order to fund most of this project with the balance being funded with capital contributions from both Acme and Gekko. The project broke ground during the latter part of 2006 but experienced a number of delays during the following two years. By the time it neared completion, the market had soured due to the 2008 recession, leaving the property entirely without pre-sales. Both loans went into default and Gekko went on the offensive against Acme for the loss of invested funds.

Specifically, Gekko accused Acme of misappropriating funds from this joint venture project to cover costs of some of Acme's other ongoing projects. The basis for these claims resided in the manner in which Acme had maintained the books and records for its projects, including this joint venture. After nearly eight years of litigation and well over a million dollars in attorney and accounting fees, Acme settled for a fraction of the damages sought by Gekko.

My team and I were engaged by Acme in order to account for the flow of funds used in the joint venture project. Every dollar drawn from loan disbursements was to be allocated against the project's budgeted hard and soft costs. We found, however, that some of the funds were being allocated to expenditures benefiting more than one of the active projects. There were also a number of *due* to and *due from* accounts reflecting payables and receivables, respectively, between the joint venture project and some of the other Acme projects. It was both the appearance and de facto commingling of funds from different projects that gave Gekko the justification and evidential ammunition to argue misappropriation.

Our combing through the accounting records and respective analyses revealed that nearly all of the funds in question were utilized for the joint venture project. Our investigation also exposed that it was the deficiency in how the books were maintained that gave rise to Gekko's claims. Had the project been better managed in terms of its accounting and related documents, then this expensive litigation may have been avoided.

Unfortunately, the case with Acme is not a rarity when it comes to real estate development projects. I have been engaged on numerous matters in the context of litigation or consulting where there are similar underlying issues. Weak internal controls, lack of documentation, commingling of funds, and deficient accounting books can all give rise to litigation, and erode management's ability to make more informed and timely decisions.

There are a number of best practices that can be implemented to give better and more timely information for decision makers, enhance transparency for stakeholders, enable tax mitigation strategies, and thwart chances of litigation.

Best Practice #1: Separately Account for Each Project
Each project has its own deadlines, budgets, plans, and requirements. Commingling the activities of discrete projects within the same accounting and other business records can impede

potential insights derived from those records. How would you ascertain how much over or under budget a project is if it is littered with expenses allocable to another project? How do you adhere to the reporting requirements of a project's loan covenants if there are no reports that speak to only the project in question? Where do you focus your efforts for efficiently allocating resources across projects when the profitability of each is unknown?

Another real estate case I was engaged on had circled litigation after one of the family owners believed his father and siblings were receiving disproportionate proceeds from completed projects. The suspicion arose due to a lack of clarity as to how profitable each project was coupled with its source of funding and aggregation of costs. Each new development project often had different ownership structure and interest percentages and was funded through proceeds rolled over from other projects. Given that the projects were not separately accounted for, there was confusion as to how much basis each family member (business partner) had in each project.

After scoping out this pre-litigation matter, the solution was clearly a re-accounting of the discrete projects going back several years. The parties conceded to this process that, while costly, would help to avoid the much more expensive route of litigation. It would have been even more inexpensive, however, to have simply maintained separate accountings of each project throughout development.

Best Practice #2: Account with Sufficient Granularity

The normal cycle for accounting for expenditures involves entering bills into accounts payable as items are incurred. Once disbursement is made, the accounts payable balance is reduced to reflect the amount paid. A bill and its corresponding payment can be for a single good or service or for dozens or even hundreds. Sometimes vendors will opt to aggregate many goods and services onto a single bill rather than separately invoice for each. For efficiency purposes, the invoice received may be entered as a single line item in the books to avoid the time of itemizing out everything on the bill.

With larger projects and especially those financed through loans, there will often be category budgets in addition to an overall project budget. Vendors may be supplying goods and services that actually fall into more than one category so recording in total means over-reporting some while under-reporting others. This efficiency gained by maintaining the books in this surface-level fashion can reduce the ability to track category budgets. Additionally, a lack of granularity in the books can limit the degree of analytics that can be performed on financial records for identifying other insights for management. While recording every single small-dollar item is not necessary, professional judgment should be executed in order to ascertain how granular the books ought to be maintained.

Accounting with sufficient granularity is also a mechanism for management to maximize tax mitigation strategies through cost segregation. Real property assets are generally depreciable for 27.5 years for residential rental property and 39 years for commercial structures. This means it will take 27.5 to 39 years for the cost of a property to be fully deducted through operating activities. In contrast, personal property assets have much shorter useful lives— often just 5 or 7 years—meaning they can be depreciated much quicker.

A cost segregation of real property can be conducted to carve out such personal property assets from the value of the overall property. This allows for faster depreciation of the property overall since its components are broken up into their respective lives rather than the entirety of it being depreciated for 27.5 or 39 years. By accounting with sufficient granularity, this cost segregation process can be more easily performed.

Best Practice #3: Maintain Strong Internal Controls

Real estate projects are susceptible to both fraud and occupational waste. Whether a project commands the attention of a single project accountant or necessitates its own accounting department, it is paramount that proper internal controls are designed, implemented, maintained, and periodically assessed.

Internal controls refer to the processes put in place to help ensure a project's financial, operational, and accounting integrity. This translates into reporting that management can rely upon in making informed business decisions during the project's life cycle. One of the most important internal controls to implement is segregation of duties. This means that more than a single individual is responsible to a particular task such as managing the disbursement of funds for project expenses. For instance, the person charged with recording expenses and reconciling the corresponding bank account is not also the same person that can authorize and sign disbursement checks.

Just because an internal control is designed and implemented does not mean that it is properly working (e.g. advocating accuracy and inhibiting fraud). If you are the business owner, a decision maker, or even a decision influencer, then you should be mindful of the efficacy of the internal controls in place. It is helpful to periodically check them to ensure processes are being followed and that the control, as designed, is operating as intended.

Best Practice #4: Regularly Review Financial and Operational Reports

The accounting for a project is not just a compliance exercise. There is a wealth of information contained in a well-documented set of books. To garner the full value of the time and attention put into these financial records, it is important to regularly review its relevant reports. In addition to tracking what the various hard and soft costs are in terms of budgets, customizable and automated reports can be designed to meet the other areas of focus for management.

The matter involving Acme would have likely been avoided if management had implemented and adhered to these best practices. Even if Gekko had still sought to go after their former venture partner, Acme's attorneys would have been able to push toward settlement much quicker if they had better accounting records and related documentation to substantiate their position. Furthermore, employing these best practices could have given Acme better line-of-sight on the status of the project including the cost of delays and lack of pre-sales. Earlier consideration of these may have afforded management a less costly exit to the project rather than default on both loans.

Every real estate project is unique and has its own myriad of factors at play. These best practices, however, are generally applicable to all such projects and provide value to management and other stakeholders. They may also serve to help prevent litigation, improve chances of successful litigation for a plaintiff, and strengthen the defense for a defendant. By implementing these best practices, a developer, investor, or owner of a real estate investment project implements can also garner some peace of mind.

CHAPTER 7

HOW TO HIRE YOUR GENERAL CONTRACTOR

By **JOE GLAESER**

Few things can be as difficult and consequential as hiring your general contractor. Although the market in recent years has suffered from a lack of good general contractors, there are certainly good ones out there—and you want to be teamed up with one of those good ones. Otherwise disaster awaits you. But no matter who you hire, the fact that you are hiring a general contractor means that the next few months of your life will be filled with difficult decisions. You'll have to overcome a huge learning curve and pay some very big bills, adding up to a potentially large amount of stress. It is very important to hire a professional general contractor who you work and communicate very well with.

Before you start, have a talk with yourself. Make sure that you are beginning the project with realistic expectations. In my experience, it is unrealistic expectations that have led to the most problems and troubles with a project. No matter how amazing of a general contractor you hire, they do not come with a magic wand. They must follow all the same stubs and protocols that we all do. Again, it is essential to have realistic expectations from the very beginning. Start by knowing that you will spend a certain amount of money and that the project is going to take a certain amount of time, and then you will not be let down in the end. If you can maintain effective communication, you can, in fact, count on those things.

Now that you have a preliminary budget in mind and you've wrapped your head around how long your project is going to take … well? What next? How do you find somebody to actually build the thing you want to build? How do you go about making sure you're hiring the right person? Good news! By the time you finish reading this chapter, you will know how to answer those questions– or, better yet, how to hire the right general contractor for your job.

There are a couple key factors to consider when selecting your general contractor. The first is their level of quality. You want to know what the general contractor is capable of in relation to their workmanship. The next is their price point (which is in direct relationship to their level of quality and workmanship). Finally, you want to consider their management skills, which will have the largest impact on their pricing, quality, and workmanship.

Quality speaks for itself. You want to hire a contractor who has a proven track record of good quality. This can be verified by asking the contractor for pictures of past work, as well as for a list of contacts for past clients. Call them to ask about the level of quality and workmanship that the contractor performed on their job. If possible, visit sites of jobs that the general contractor has in progress and inspect their work. Most general contractors will be more than happy to share their past performance with you. If they aren't happy, consider it a big red flag and run as quickly as possible.

The next major point is management. Your project will ultimately be a success or a failure due to the management of the project. It cannot be stated strongly enough the management of the job is everything. There are many companies who simply will send their crews out to a job site, tell them what to do, and only periodically check in. Run away from these companies as fast as you can. When you interview your contractor, ask if they have constant on-site management. Only hire a company that provides that service. It is imperative that, no matter how big or small the job is, a company has constant on-site supervision. There are a tremendous number of variables in a given project, which means there are so many things that can go wrong. You do not want to find yourself in a position where you are talking to tradesmen and laborers and asking them questions that should be handled by people with much greater expertise.

Another reason why on-site supervision is so important is quality. An on-site superintendent or project manager has the ability to inspect the work as it's being done. Should they see that something is not being completed properly they can stop the process right then and there and correct the issue immediately, thus saving a massive amount of time and money. Without someone providing feedback in real time, the problem would go unseen and uncorrected until the end; at that point, to correct anything, you'd have to remove finishes and work backwards, translating into time and money lost.

Issues only compound the longer a problem goes undetected or the longer a quality issue sits unresolved. And what does that mean? More time and money that didn't need to be spent if the problem had been corrected immediately on the spot—that is, had a general contractor with constant on-site supervision been hired. Clients who try to save a buck with a subpar contractor will inevitably pay for it in the end. It's much better—and cheaper—to pay a weekly salary for a superintendent or project manager on-site rather than, at the end of a project, going back and correcting a thousand things that could've been caught right away.

There's also the issue of subcontractor coordination. Dealing with subcontractors—coordinating their schedules, their workflow, negotiating their contracts—is a full-time job in and of itself. The project superintendent should handle all those issues anyway, as he or she knows what's best for the project. In addition to full-time project management, you want to make sure that the contractor himself will have a direct hand in the overall project management.

When you interview your potential general contractors, ask them these questions and be ready to hold them accountable throughout the course of the project:

How many times a week will you be stopping by the site to inspect progress?

Will there be full-time on-site supervision and is it the same person every day?

Will you be providing daily and weekly status updates and reports?

A good general contractor will answer these questions to your satisfaction, which will in turn build a level of confidence and trust in you as the homeowner. You will be happier with the end result.

The final issue is pricing. In my opinion and experience, there is only one way that anybody should ever do budgeting and billing: cost-plus. Ninety-nine percent of contractors provide a lump sum number for their bid. Which leaves a lot of questions: Where did this number come from? What does it entail? This is by far the number one reason why people don't trust their contractor. They have no clue as to what goes into the price. All they see is a big lump sum number which can occasionally be broken down into different categories of work with smaller lump sum numbers. But, again, many homeowners have no clue as to what is going into calculating those numbers.

Conversely, in a cost-plus budget, you know where every penny is going: every dollar spent is accounted for and proven with receipts. In the cost-plus method, the contractor provides a budget up-front with estimates of what things will cost. Then, as the work is performed, he provides the client with the total of his itemized invoices and receipts and adds a contractor fee—normally a percentage of the total—on top of it all. At the end of the day, you know how every dollar is being spent, including how much overhead and profit is charged on the project. In my opinion, this is the only way to hire a contractor. When every bill comes with proof and explanation as to how that invoice was calculated, you can have total trust and confidence in your general contractor.

There are many contractors out there and it can be hard to find the best one for you to work with. If you are patient and ask the right questions, you'll find the right one. Don't compromise on your expectations. Remember that you're the boss—and you're the one who signs the checks.

CHAPTER 8

PRACTICAL ADVICE FROM A REAL ESTATE INVESTOR WITH A BAR CARD

By **JOHN FAGERHOLM**

"An investment in knowledge pays the best interest."
—Benjamin Franklin

I am an expert in business and real estate. I don't make that claim lightly. And surely there are people that know much more than me about topics in both fields. However, I have spent almost two decades representing entrepreneurs and CEOs of companies and I have witnessed the successes and failures of thousands of highly productive and intelligent people. I receive an education every day on how money is made and invested. I have learned what works and what doesn't work both from their experiences as well as from my own personal wins and losses. What do all of these winners have in common? Real estate. It doesn't matter the industry these people are in: They all have some form of real estate in their portfolios and I get to see it all without ever risking my own money. A practical guide to the do's and do not's in real estate would fill much more than a chapter in a book so I will narrow them down to the ten general but important lessons I think will help you make money in real estate and avoid losing all of it in a costly lawsuit.

"The best investment on Earth is earth."
—Louis Glickman

Lesson 1. **Figure out your objectives before investing.** We have all been in the situation where a friend or family member tells us about this unbelievable real estate opportunity that we just have to invest in and we should do it right away before the opportunity is lost. *I would rather pass up a good deal then enter into a bad one.* There will always be a good deal that fits your real estate investing goals around the corner—but there might be a bad one in front of you right now. You are not missing out by blindly investing into someone else's dream. Figure out exactly, to the smallest detail, what criteria you want before ever putting a dollar into real estate. For example, I currently only invest in B and C properties, 60 units or more, in states that have good landlord-tenant laws and in cities that have a growing population and a strong blue collar job market. Nothing else, ever.

"We must all hang together or we will surely hang separately."
—Benjamin Franklin

Lesson 2. **Build a team of experts.** Real estate is a team sport. You need people around you that can do things you cannot do. Even if you dedicate all of your time, you will never be able to be an expert in the many moving parts that must be addressed when investing in real estate. At minimum, your team should consist of a broker that specializes in your criteria; a loan officer that specializes in your criteria; and a lawyer that specializes in real estate in the jurisdiction you are investing. Only deal with good people. Bad people do bad things. They can't help themselves. The fastest way to a lawsuit is to be involved with shady people. (See my introduction to this book.)

> *"If it don't make dollars, it don't make sense."*
> —D.J. Quik

Lesson 3. **Be a cash flow investor.** Cash flow is the only guarantee you have. Equity comes and goes at the whim of the market. This is one of the hardest lessons to learn. I made this mistake between 2004 and 2008 along with millions of other investors. Equity was increasing monthly and I was buying any condo in Los Angeles and Las Vegas I could get my hands on. My thought was that even if the market crashed, I would just keep increasing the rents. Long story short: I invested at the only time in history that equity and rents fell at the same time. Usually, when people stop buying, rents go up because more people are renting. A classic inverse relationship. However, in 2008 so many people defaulted at the same time that the banks could not foreclose fast enough and people were in their homes free for two to four years so it caused the rental market to collapse. There was more real estate litigation between 2008 and 2012 then any other period in history. Equity investors were double losers because they lost equity and were litigating against banks for unpaid mortgages. Meanwhile, cash flow investors quietly collected their rents.

"Every battle is won or lost before it is ever fought."
—Sun Tzu

Lesson 4. **Do your research.** Research the properties you are interested in buying; research the neighborhoods you like; and research everyone that you are doing business with. It is my experience that the people with the most information make the best deals. Those that leave anything to chance are at risk of overpaying or worse–buying something that will cost them in the end. A few years ago, I broke several of my own rules by buying a house in Detroit sight unseen based on a description and old pictures on the internet. I didn't know the city, the neighborhood, or anyone in Detroit. When I went to see the house a few months later with a contractor, it was in a dilapidated and abandoned neighborhood. What's worse, someone had burned my house down shortly before I arrived. It was still smoldering when I showed up. No one called the fire department, no one investigated ownership, and no one informed me. All I could do was laugh at myself. You learn the most from expensive lessons.

"If you are brave enough to say goodbye,
life will reward you with a new hello."
—Paulo Coelho

Lesson 5. **Plan with an exit strategy in mind.** Successful investors make their money when they buy real estate, not when they sell it. This topic is a book itself so I will try to make it clear in a few sentences. Your options for an exit are usually sell or refinance and you do one or the other depending on the particular situation. Every exit strategy is determined by one, the identified risks of the acquisition; two, maximizing returns; and three, agreements with third parties. If you purchase a property and you know that there will be large expenses in seven years—like replacing a roof—those expenses would be identified risks. You may have an exit strategy of selling the property after year five. Another example is even if you intend to hold the property for a long period, you may have an exit strategy of refinancing the property because either you think you can get a better interest rate later, or your equity is increasing and you want to use some of that money for other opportunities. If your deal has investors attached, a good exit strategy would be to either sell or refinance as soon as you have met the promised returns. Not only does this free you from the burden of investors but it frees you to seek other opportunities if you sell or earn great returns on your own by buying out the investors with a refinance strategy.

> *"He should've read the contract closer before he signed,*
> *but being moments from a painful and violent death*
> *provided a necessary sense of urgency."*
> —Andrea Laurence, Sexy As Hell

Lesson 6. **Get everything in writing.** In real estate, there is a common law that exists in every jurisdiction called the *statute of frauds*. This law requires certain types of contracts including real estate contracts to be in writing to be enforceable. It doesn't matter if it is a family member or the love of your life; if its real property your deal must be in writing to be enforced. No exceptions. True story: When I was a fairly new attorney I helped a friend of mine with a real estate problem. He had been living with a much younger woman for the better part of a decade. During their relationship, they bought a condo using his money but her credit. The condo was in her name because of his bad credit but he paid all the costs of the condo. In fact, we could not find one instances where she contributed even one penny into the property. Eventually, she left him for a younger man and tried to evict him from the property because she wanted to sell it. Because he did not have anything in writing and the property was not in his name, there was nothing he could do. The end result was not "fair," as we would say in layman terms.

> *"Winning isn't the only thing, it's everything."*
> —Vince Lombardi

Lesson 7. **Win-win or lose-lose.** If someone doesn't win in a deal it means they have lost. This is a dangerous position for everyone in a business transaction because the loser could potentially cause legal problems. In America, anyone can sue for anything and it is my experience that most lawsuits stem from personal issues and not business-related disputes. If everyone doesn't win, everyone will lose in a lawsuit. I am a big believer in setting out expectations up front and making sure everyone receives what was expected. In some instances, deals change but even then, it is better to either adjust everyone's expectations or to even reduce your take so that everyone else is happy. This will save you time and money in the long run.

> *"Any problem, big or small, always seems to start with bad communication."*
> —Emma Thompson

Lesson 8. **Communicate, communicate, communicate.** If a real estate deal is good, it will sell itself. People tend to exaggerate the upside of a deal and minimize the potential risks. This is a huge mistake. You must *clearly* communicate in *writing* all of the potential risks. If anything goes wrong with the deal or the deal does not produce as expected, the potential of a civil lawsuit or worse, criminal indictment is very high. All deals have their hiccups and most investors understand the risks if you communicate with them regularly and give them both the good and the bad upfront. If things do not go as expected, it will be your good communication, and the risks that you disclosed up front, that will save you from a potential legal problem.

> *"Speak softly and carry a big stick."*
> —Theodore Roosevelt

Lesson 9. **Build your war chest.** Litigation is inevitable in American business life. Embrace it. We have the most litigious business environment in the world–in the United States, there is one lawyer for every 300 people. You must be prepared for a fight at all times. Money is ammunition in litigation. Money dictates how good your lawyer is going to be, how many lawyers you can use, and how long you can fight. I recommend a two-prong strategy: one, have litigation insurance ready for any defense that you may need to mount against an attacker; and two, set aside a small annual budget for your company and for each project in case you need to be the aggressor. I have sued plenty of times over a real estate deal and I have found that is the best way to get someone's attention when they are being less than cooperative. Also, sometimes people are just bad people and need to be sued. I once sued my (now ex) mother-in-law over real estate. That sounds ridiculous, but I was justified. It was the second time she breached a real estate agreement with me assuming that since I was married to her daughter she could get away with it. The first time she breached, it cost me somewhere between $75-$100k and I certainly wasn't going to absorb another loss without a fight. I estimate about $30,000 later for her ($0 for me, since I represented myself), she waived the white flag. Every smart real estate investor should have this kind of litigation resource at the ready.

> *"So it's true, when all is said and done,*
> *grief is the price we pay for love."*
> —E.A Bucchianeri

Lesson 10. **Never fall in love with a deal.** This was the hardest lesson for me to learn. I am a hopeless romantic when it comes to a sexy piece of property. Anything with a spiral staircase … *mmm*. If I found a property that I could see myself living in or if it were in a neighborhood I liked, I really had a difficult time passing even if the deal did not fit my criteria. I once bought a penthouse because the loft reminded me of my dream bedroom as a kid. Luckily, that one turned out okay in the end but several others did not. Now, I am older and wiser. It doesn't matter whether I like any property because I am not investing to live in it. I am investing for my perfect tenant (which I figured out by determining my objectives in lesson one)–an employed blue collar worker.

I hope these lessons help. Remember, any warnings are to help you avoid mistakes, not to convince you to try something else. There just isn't anything better than investing over time in real estate.

CHAPTER 9

USING INSURANCE TO PROTECT REAL ESTATE

By **JORGE RABASO**

One of the most common mistakes that I have seen is people leaving things for tomorrow. This happens in financial matters, in relationships, in real estate—in short, in many of the important decisions in our lives. Sometimes I find that people know about the living benefits (critical illness) that are included in most life insurance policies, but they don't get the policy because of lack of time or because they can do it tomorrow. What they don't remember is that if their health changes, or even if they pass away, tomorrow will be too late and their family will have to deal with the mortgage and all the debts. Life insurance with living benefits is not expensive and it is the best peace of mind people could ever have.

In real estate, life insurance and disability insurance plays an essential role. Your home is one of the biggest investments you'll ever make, which is why families carrying a mortgage often need both life insurance and disability insurance. If one of the breadwinners dies, a life insurance payout can help the family keep up with mortgage payments and stay in the home.

What would happen if you had an accident and couldn't work anymore? The answer is disability insurance. What would happen if you get sick? Or if you pass away? The answer is life insurance with living benefits.

About Disability Insurance

Although most of us are aware of the need for health insurance coverage when managing our financial risk, many of us fail to consider the possibility that we could become disabled. A disability income insurance policy can help replace income lost because of an injury or illness. Few people would have an adequate "war chest" for an extended health battle and subsequent loss of income. Unfortunately, many of us will need disability income protection before we retire. Without the appropriate coverage, a disability could spell financial disaster.

Disability at any age can disrupt income while medical expenses mount. Unless you have a battle plan, the effects of even a short-term disability could be financially debilitating and emotionally devastating. If you become disabled and are unable to work, the benefits provided by disability insurance can help replace a portion of your earned income. The appropriate amount of disability coverage will depend on your situation.

First, consider carrying enough coverage to replace at least 60 percent of your earnings. Many companies limit benefits to between 50 and 80 percent of all sources of disability income prior to the disability. This would mean, for example, that the amount of any Social Security disability payments you receive could be deducted from your benefit amount.

If you are concerned about the cost of a private disability insurance policy, consider extending the waiting period, which is the time between the onset of the disability and when you start receiving benefits. Choosing a 90-day or 180-day waiting period (instead of 30 days) may help lower your premium. Be sure to compare and review policy benefits carefully. Disability insurance can be an affordable way to help protect your assets in the event of a disability. One of your greatest assets is the ability to earn an income. If you were to lose that ability due to a disabling accident or illness, how would you pay your bills, your mortgage, send your kids to college, and save for retirement?

Weigh Your Options

When evaluating disability income insurance policies, it's helpful to consider the following.

Definition of disability. You can typically choose between "own occupation" coverage and "any occupation" coverage. With "any occupation" coverage, you can claim disability only if you are unable to perform any type of job. This type of coverage is generally less expensive than "own occupation" coverage.

Amount of monthly coverage. You can purchase disability insurance that will replace a certain percentage of your income—normally up to 50 or 60 percent of your pre-disability income. You should purchase coverage that will enable you to meet your monthly financial obligations.

Waiting period. The waiting period represents the amount of time that must pass between the date you become disabled and the date that disability income payments begin. The longer the waiting period, the less expensive coverage will be.

Benefit period. The benefit period can range from several months to life. The longer the benefit period, the higher the cost of insurance.

A disability income insurance policy could make the difference between financial security and financial hardship. Don't wait to consider this protection until it's too late.

About Life Insurance

Most people don't know that life insurance products now include "living benefits" that cover critical, chronic and terminal illnesses. With modern technology and with the rapid advances in medical science, many of today's critical illnesses could be cured within a lifetime. If your life insurance includes "living benefits" you can take part of your death benefits as a lump sum to cover the income you need during the treatment period of your critical illness. And this is tax free. You will be able to pay your liabilities and have the money that you need. You can request of the insurance company different sums according to your needs.

Critical Illness

A life insurance policy with a critical illness rider, or addition, will pay out a lump-sum benefit to the insured if they are diagnosed with a covered critical condition (such as cancer, stroke, or coma). This benefit is accelerated from your death benefit. Think about the peace of mind that you will have knowing that you can protect your assets and your family if you get a critical illness.

Chronic Illness

Chronic illness insurance is a rider, or addition, to your standard life insurance (or mortgage protection) policy. It pays for medical care and non-medical care that your health insurance does not cover. Chronic illness insurance may be more frequently utilized as more and more people become at greater risk of developing a chronic illness due to a poor diet, lack of exercise, or weight issues. Many aspects of the modern Western lifestyle will put you at greater risk of getting a chronic illness even if you are young. A chronic illness is one that lasts for a lifetime. The illness or condition cannot be cured and doesn't go away on its own. In addition to requiring ongoing medical treatment, you may also need help doing necessary daily activities. The six activities that people with chronic illness are most likely to have problems with are called Activities of Daily Living, or ADLs. The chronic illness rider pays you if you have been diagnosed with a chronic illness and you are unable to perform at least two of the Activities of Daily Living.

The six ADLs are:
- **Bathing:** get into and out of the bathtub, wash, brush teeth, shave, or perform other grooming activities

- **Dressing:** pull clothes on, fasten buttons, or close zippers

- **Eating:** manage the silverware to eat independently

- **Transferring:** walk or otherwise transfer from the bed to a wheelchair and back

- **Toileting:** get on and off the toilet without help

- **Continence:** control bladder and bowel function

Terminal Illness

Many life insurance companies offer a terminal illness rider. Such a rider allows the insured to use a portion of their death benefit while they are still alive if a doctor deems the policyholder terminally ill. Terminal illness riders are usually included with most life insurance policies at no additional cost; however, some life insurance companies have riders that allow even more flexibility in using death benefit while the insured member is still alive.

Types of Life Insurance

People very often assume that life insurance is very expensive and they don't even ask for a quote. There are many kinds of policies, and indeed, most of the time they are very affordable. According to my experience, we should think about it this way: "It is not life insurance that I want. Because I will live until I'm 100 years old, what I really need to have is the peace of mind that I'm covering the people that I love."

These are the kinds of life insurance that you could consider.

Term Life Insurance

Term life insurance is the most basic and usually the most affordable. Policies can be purchased for a specified period of time. If you die within the time period defined in your policy, the insurance company will pay your beneficiaries the face value of your policy. Policies can usually be bought for one to 30-year time spans. Annual renewable term insurance usually can be renewed every year without proof of insurability, but the premium may increase with each renewal. Term insurance is useful if you can afford only a low-cost option or you need life insurance only for a certain amount of time (such as until your children graduate from college).

Permanent Life Insurance

The other major category is permanent life insurance. You pay a premium for as long as you live, and a benefit will be paid to your beneficiaries upon your death. Permanent life insurance typically comes with a "cash value" savings element. There are three main types of permanent life insurance: whole, universal, and variable.

Whole Life Insurance

This type of permanent life insurance has a premium that stays the same throughout the life of the policy. Although the premiums may seem higher than the risk of death in the early years, they can accumulate cash value and are invested in the company's general investment portfolio. You may be able to borrow funds from the cash value or surrender your policy for its face value, if necessary. Access to cash values through borrowing or partial surrenders can reduce the policy's cash value and death benefit, increase the chance that the policy will lapse, and may result in a tax liability if the policy terminates before the death of the insured. Additional out-of-pocket payments may be needed if actual dividends or investment returns decrease, if you withdraw policy values, if you take out a loan, or if current charges increase.

Universal Life Insurance

Universal life coverage goes one step further. You have the same type of coverage and cash value as you would with whole life insurance, but with greater flexibility. Once money has accumulated in your cash-value account, you may be able to vary the frequency, as well as the amount, of your premiums. In fact, it may be possible to structure the policy so that the invested cash value eventually covers your premium costs completely. Of course, it's important to remember that altering your premiums may decrease the value of the death benefit.

Index Universal Life Insurance

With Index Life Insurance, you receive the same death protection as with other types of permanent life insurance, but you are given the control over how your cash value is invested. You have the option of investing your cash value in different strategies based on the S&P 500 Index. The value of your policy has the potential to grow more quickly. The strategies pay up to 12 percent based on the index but they have the floor of zero percent. This means that you are protected against the crash of the market. The premiums for this type of insurance are fixed and you cannot change them in relation to the size of your cash-value account.

Using Life Insurance to Fund Your Real Estate Deals

Did you know that you can use a life insurance policy as a funding mechanism for your real estate deals? And that your policy can serve as a very low-interest, or even no interest, source of funds? And that the money inside your policy grows tax-free? And is protected from creditors? And that it is a phenomenal way to build wealth, not only for yourself, but for your children and grandchildren?

I have been in the insurance business for more than 20 years and I have good news and bad news for you. The good news is that the information you have just read is what will really give you the peace of mind you need to live better. The bad news is that only 20 percent of the readers of this chapter will do something about it. Do you know why? Because this is important but not urgent! You could leave this for tomorrow. Or the day after that. If you got this far, you might as well take the next step and pick up the phone and call me or call your agent. You will wake up tomorrow with the peace of mind of being covered and knowing that the mortgage will be paid if something happens to you. It is the peace of mind you and your family need—and deserve.

The illustration provided is for information use only. Because I do not provide legal or tax advice, you should consult your Accountant or Attorney before making any decision. I am a CALIFORNIA licensed Insurance broker and my license number is 0A96977

CHAPTER 10

SHORT TERM RENTALS OVERVIEW:
Airbnb

By **LUIS GUAJARDO**

If you have ever thought about acquiring or transforming real estate into a rental property using short term rental sites like Airbnb, here is a thumbnail sketch about what you should consider to maximize ROI as you manage real estate. In the right city, an Airbnb can earn a higher return of investment (ROI) as a rental income property than a traditional long-term rental. You will have to put in a lot more blood, sweat, and tears to managing the rental property, but if executed correctly, you will reap the rewards. Besides hard work, factors that determine whether an Airbnb is the right investment for you include its location, seasonality, and local laws and regulations.

When managing an Airbnb, you can do it yourself, or hire a management company.

The do it yourself approach requires a lot more work researching, decorating, marketing and advertising, building a team to run operations and guest relations, and accounting. Additionally, this time cost might limit your ability to scale as you add multiple properties into your portfolio. The upside is that you keep every penny you earn.

For some people, hiring a property management company may be the better option. They take all the work out of the equation, and you collect a check every month. This in turn allows you to more easily scale as you increase the number of properties in your portfolio. If you are going to trust a company to manage your asset and the revenue that comes from it, then you better be sure they are competent and have the resources in place to make sure that you are maximizing your revenue.

Single Family Homes and Condos

Single family homes and condos are popular choices for rental income properties. Traditionally one of these would be bought, renovated, and put on the market to lease to a long-term tenant. Returns can range from 5 to 12 percent. I have heard of some anomalies where long term rental properties can get an 18 percent return, but in most cases, that's not common (All these estimates assume the property is bought with cash. The ROI on financed properties gets a bit more complicated).

By turning a long-term rental into Airbnb rental, your returns can grow to anywhere from 12 to 40 percent. The annual gross revenue you can earn is anywhere from one and a half to two times the fair market rent value of a long-term lease.

Typically, the value of a single family home is based on the recent sales price of other homes in the surrounding area. Since the value of a single family home is based on its surrounding area, high-volume tourist areas are good candidates for an Airbnb investment because both the cash flow and annual appreciation value are predictable and positive.

A good example of this is Tulum, Mexico, where the tourist volume is increasing at remarkable rates. This, in turn, has pushed the value of real estate up an average of seven percent per year, in addition to the cash flow the tourist industry provides to rental properties.

The equity of your home can also be affected by turning your rental property into an Airbnb. For the right buyer—like an investor looking for a rental income property—a strong revenue history can help boost the value of your home.

Multifamily Real Estate

Multifamily unit properties are unique because not only can you earn more cash on a building that is converted to Airbnb, you also can instantly increase the selling value of your building. The value of multi-unit buildings is based more on the rental income it is generating than a price comparison of what other properties sell for in the area.

There are several reasons why multifamily properties are good real estate investments:

1. **Cash flow.** Multifamily units, for the most part, generate higher monthly income than single family homes.

2. **Control.** You control the entire building. There are no other owners or an HOA that require decisions to be passed by a majority.

3. **Tax advantages.** It's not what you gross; it's the net revenue you earn, and real estate offers tremendous tax benefits.

4. **Economy of scale.** This is a huge advantage when trying to scale your business. It is easier to manage one entire building than multiple single-family homes scattered about a city.

5. **Ability to force appreciation.** The value is not as reliant on comparable properties as it is your ability to increase the value through growing the net operating income (NOI).

6. **Velocity of money.** This refers to the ability to refinance a property, withdraw the equity, maintain control of the asset, and invest the refinanced proceeds into another property. An Airbnb can be instrumental to increase the loan amount you are approved for as it will be based on the Net Operating Income (NOI).

The capitalization rate (cap rate), is the ratio of Net Operating Income (NOI) to property asset value. The standard cap rate can be anywhere from 4 to 10 percent depending on how high demand the area is. So, for example, if a property recently sold for $1,000,000 and had an NOI of $60,000, then the cap rate would be $60,000/$1,000,000, or 6 percent.

This is where converting your rental income property into an Airbnb can be a game changer. If the same property above was at a 6 percent cap rate as a traditional long term multifamily rental property, and based on a 12 to 40 percent increase in your NOI, your cap rate could change from that 6 percent to anywhere between 7 percent and 10 percent virtually overnight.

How to Maximize the Return on Your Airbnb

There are key factors that will push the ROI of your Airbnb to higher percentages. They include:

1. **Location.** Market research can help determine whether a city is a good candidate for an Airbnb, and where to invest within that city.

2. **Seasonality.** Market research will also determine if a city has extreme seasonality or a long "low season" which will have an impact on your cash flow and overall revenue performance.

3. **Local Legislation.** Some cities ban Airbnbs while others highly regulate. You need to find out if any local legislation or HOA bylaws will inhibit your revenue earning potential.

4. **Furnishing and Interior Design.** How you furnish your Airbnb–considering sleep occupancy and design style

in relation to your target audience—is a huge factor in its revenue earning potential.

5. **Marketing/Advertising.** Working knowledge of the available third party channels (Airbnb, Homeaway, etc.) is crucial to maximizing revenue and occupancy rates. Post professional photos, a well-written description, and develop a clear pricing strategy.

6. **Inquiry response.** Fast/immediate responses get the highest conversion rates confirming reservations.

7. **Operations.** Efficiency is key with operations. Keep your overhead and general costs low while perusing quality services for guests that encourage good reviews.

8. **Risk management.** Minimize liabilities such as older or defective appliances or amenities and keep the Airbnb up on safety standards to minimize partial refunds. Manage payments appropriately to minimize credit card chargebacks and fraud. And file damage claims when guests are negligent and damage the property, furniture, or amenities.

Location

Location is one of the top two factors that affect revenues (sleep occupancy is the other).

There are important things to look for when analyzing if a property is in a good location which can negatively or positively affect your reviews.

1. **Pay attention to traffic.** No one likes to sit in traffic so avoid high traffic areas if you can. Consider if an area is walkable and close to public transportation (especially subways or trains).

2. **Proximity to major tourist attractions, landmarks, business centers, or activities.** Most of your guests will be on vacation (unless your property is specifically geared toward business travelers) so consider proximity to major attractions, including proximity to shopping, restaurants, and nightlife. People on vacation spend money and go out to eat; shopping, restaurants, and nightlife are useful to have in close proximity to your property.

3. **Proximity to Neighbors.** Who are your neighbors? Vacation rentals can be a bit noisier than units with a long-term tenant. Take your neighbors into consideration—they could become a pain to deal with and negatively impact your reviews.

4. **Proximity to construction.** No one likes to wake up at 8 a.m. to construction noise. Take care to notice the surrounding environment of your potential property. If you see empty lots, or broken-down houses, make sure to ask the realtor if plans to build are in the foreseeable future.

Seasonality

Evaluating areas to invest in when your target is property intended for vacation rentals, can include several data points to pay attention to but the easiest and most readily available information on the internet is hotel data. Hotels and the search engine sites built around the industry give key indications of seasonality, occupancy rates, and average daily rates (ADR). Pricing is updated regularly online to adjust to demand in order to maximize the occupancy rates and total annual revenue. By comparing the ADR to the occupancy rate, you'll get what is called Rev Par—the true average daily rate based on how many days each room is booked. The Rev Par will give you a broad idea of what to project for room revenues factoring in seasonality.

Local Legislation and Regulations

Local governments have reacted differently to the explosion of Airbnb around the world. Some local governments embrace Airbnb. Many cities suffer from a shortage of hotels and cannot meet the demand for accommodations, so the emergence of Airbnb and other short-term rental companies helps solve this problem and brings in more tourist revenue. These cities and states should be the first locations you target.

Unfortunately, some local governments do not look at short term rentals the same way. Instead of embracing the opportunities Airbnb can open for a city, bureaucrats argue that the proliferation of Airbnb negatively affects the price of rentals for residents that are looking for long-term leases. They also cite safety concerns and lack of tax regulation. These cities should be avoided as they often have laws that regulate Airbnb rentals with fines or the amount of nights legally allowed to book short term rentals.

Zoning Laws

In other cities, local legislators manage the regulation of short term rentals for multi-family or single-family properties by using zoning regulations. If the property is not zoned for short-term rentals, then the property cannot be rented on a short-term basis. Often, a violation results in fines and may increase significantly with each additional infraction. Typically, vacation destinations welcome tourists, but have zoning laws in place to control the areas and number of vacation rentals that exist.

The definition of a "short term rental" varies by town, city, and county. In most cities, a short-term rental is defined as anything occupied for less than one month. If the property is within a city border, then it is governed by the city's zoning laws. If the property is not within any city, like in an unincorporated part of the county, then it is governed by the county's zoning laws.

Different zones will offer different permissions for rental properties, and might differ from city to city. For example, a property which is zoned R-1 (Residential-1) may allow short-term rentals in one city but not another. Larger buildings are often zoned for mixed commercial and residential use and are typically good opportunities. The best way to determine the permitted uses of a property is to check with the planning and zoning department of the city.

Some of the biggest zoning battles are happening in popular vacation spots like Hawaii, Arizona, Nevada, and Florida. In some places, short-term rentals have been prohibited in residential areas for years. In other areas, however, short term rental restrictions are new. Recent law changes are typically driven by year-round residents who don't want vacationers rotating in and out of their neighborhood.

If you purchase a property where Airbnbs are prohibited, your options are very limited. In some cases, you may be able to obtain a special non-conforming use permit from the zoning department to legally rent your property short-term. In other cases, your only option is to attempt to change the actual zoning of the property. Both options are typically time-consuming and expensive.

Enforcement of these zoning rules vary, but in many areas, zoning officers usually don't search for zoning violators. Most enforcement actions result from a disgruntled neighbor reporting a violation to the zoning department. That action will most likely include an order to cease and desist short-term renting the property immediately or incur daily fines.

Keep in mind that the zoning laws are different and separate from tax laws. If zoning rules prohibit short-term renting but you choose to take your chances and short-term rent, you will still be liable for sales and lodging taxes. Additionally, "short-term" is usually defined differently in zoning ordinances as it is in tax ordinances. In Florida, for example, zoning ordinances typically define short-term as anything less than 30 consecutive days, but tax laws define short-term as anything less than or equal to six consecutive months. So you may rent "long-term" as defined by zoning laws, but still owe sales and lodging taxes if you're renting "short-term" as defined by tax laws.

Furnishing and Interior Design

Sleep occupancy is the number one factor in revenue performance. The two key factors in sleep occupancy are bedroom count and bed count. The layout of your rental can have a huge influence on your overall revenue performance.

For example, a property that has two bedrooms will perform better if the master bedroom has a King or Queen bed and the guest room has two full beds, allowing the property to sleep six people. That extra bed allows for guests to split the cost of the rental between more people therefore raising the value of your property. An extra bed can equate to a 10 to 15 percent boost in your monthly revenue.

You'll see an even greater boost in revenue by adding an extra room. If you turn a two-bedroom property into a three-bedroom property, the value added is even greater than you'd gain by adding an extra bed. An extra room can equate to up to a 20 to 40 percent boost in your monthly revenue.

When considering the style of your interior design, your strategy should be female pro and male neutral. If you can design your rental so that females like it and males can tolerate it, then you are golden. For example, most women won't like a bachelor-pad style home and won't want to book it. Your audience is now cut down to groups of males (most likely bachelors). On the opposite end, women might love a pink palace style home, but many men will not. Again, you lose out on families where two members of the opposite sex are the decision makers; you've limited your audience.

Stick to female pro/male neutral, and you will attract a larger audience. The key point is that you are keeping the design fairly neutral to appeal to the greatest number of people. This strategy should be maintained throughout the design process. The more you commit to a specific style, the more you narrow your audience. Be minimalistic when furnishing your rental. In my experience, people prefer rentals that feel similar to a hotel. A minimalistic rental is easier to keep clean and also appears cleaner. Keep your rental bright with light colors and keep it clean with clutter out of site.

Marketing/Advertising

Even with a well-designed Airbnb in a prime spot, a poor marketing strategy could inhibit your earnings potential. Advertise on websites beside Airbnb, including Homeaway, Trip Advisor, and Booking.com, to name a few. For multifamily units with smaller and lower valued units, Airbnb and Booking.com may perform better than Homeaway or Flipkey. The converse is also true.

Once you choose the best channels to market your property on, you must build content suited to attract that audience. Use professional photographers, proper staging, and quality lighting to build your listing. Take time to write accurate and descriptive words to help sell your Airbnb.

Pricing

The industry has evolved quickly and hosts have become educated in dynamic pricing strategies often used by hotels to maximize revenue and occupancy rates. There are several tools out there to help automate this process.

Operations

Operations encompasses all that occurs after the reservation is confirmed. The guest experience is a crucial part of the rental process as online reviews can make or break just about any business. Whether it's through a property management company or a team you put together yourself, make sure to hire quality cleaners, maintenance workers, and administrators to ensure a smooth experience from check in to check out.

Risk Management

Risk management refers to everything that could lose you money. This could be botched operations or maintenance issues with the property that result in guest refunds. It could be listing inaccurate content that results in partial refunds.

Risk management can also refer to safety standards. Make sure to take proper precautions with smoke/carbon monoxide detectors and fire extinguishers. Even small details like using metal garbage cans instead of plastic can play a role in protecting yourself from issues.

If a guest is hurt, sets the property on fire, or dies due to your negligence in making sure your Airbnb has proper safety precautions in place, then you leave yourself liable to legal consequences. Always make sure you have the proper insurance in place to protect yourself if something unforeseen happens.

There's a lot that goes into the successful management of an Airbnb, but when done correctly, an Airbnb can be a tremendous boost on your ROI for a real estate investment. Make sure to measure what your time is worth when determining your strategy as you grow your portfolio. Hiring internal staff, managing day-to-day operations, and accounting are all very labor intensive and may not be the best use of your time. Hiring a professional management company to outsource the daily operations makes a lot of sense when factoring in the time you would spend, but it depends on your immediate goals and what you want to be doing with your time. Either way, an Airbnb can be a great asset to add to your portfolio.

CHAPTER 11

LIFESTYLE LUXURY PROPERTIES

By **MARKUS CANTER**

Real estate transforms the lives of those who are blessed to own property. Through the ownership of the right property, real estate can help create abundance and wealth. But lifestyle and luxury properties can bring riches far beyond what can be quantified, as a beautiful home also brings joy, love, peace, and health.

If you are interested in buying and selling property or contemplating real estate as a career, this chapter will help you adjust your approach during the entire real estate transaction from start to finish. This approach has catapulted my team and I to achieve consistent results, success, and a business practice that is extremely fulfilling and exciting.

In partnership with my extraordinary wife and business partner, Cristie St. James, and with the unyielding support of our real estate team, it is our philosophy that luxury is defined by providing the highest level of service and care. Even beyond service and care, we believe that it is our ultimate privilege and responsibility to treat and consider others as family. If you consider every client as a brother, sister, cousin, uncle, or aunt, then you will naturally be committed to providing an extraordinary service experience and exceptional results.

This is the game of real estate. A quarterback doesn't make it to the Super Bowl overnight. A successful real estate business is built by focusing on one victory at a time, and it is at the culmination of every year, year after year, that the payoff is realized. I am 100 percent in service to my clients. I'm grateful to say that my clients found a payoff in every deal I've done, ending up in properties that were truly the perfect fit. I don't sell people properties—I focus on creating incredible opportunities from which my clients can choose.

When I first got into real estate, a very wise attorney told me, "You should never want a deal more than your clients do." I live by this! I receive a tremendous amount of joy by focusing on giving to others and ensuring that my client's lives are elevated through buying and selling real estate. I am present to what will fulfill them while being mindful to their needs. This combination means that the majority of my business comes from referrals.

We have represented and sold many properties designed by famous architects, including A. Quincy Jones, Lorcan O'Herlihy,

Edward Hale Fickett, William Krisel, and Ralph C. Flewelling. Recently, we represented iconic properties like Frank Sinatra's Palm Springs Desert Hideaway, Quincy Jones' 1962 Sherwood Residence, Ralph C. Flewelling's Hancock Park Property, and Brian Grazer's Malibu Colony Home. We have become globally acclaimed for our rare understanding and marketing skills geared toward unique properties. Our agency receives iconic property offers from exceptional buyers all around the world because we recognize and pay close attention to the many intricacies (like terms, conditions, purchase price, particularities, sell probability) that determine what it takes to identify and deliver the right buyer for an iconic property.

Michelangelo saw a block of marble that had been rejected on many occasions because sculptors said there was no form inside. He saw what others could not. For months Michelangelo chiseled away at the stone that others had rejected to release the figure now known as the iconic statue of David. He was the first to see, within that stone, the work of art long before it was realized. His gift was the vision and talent required to bring that vision to fruition.

Everyone has a gift in life. Just as Michelangelo trusted his vision, I encourage you to trust what your heart is telling you that you are destined to do. Vision is my greatest talent. I'm fortunate to have helped paint a picture for the lives of my clients through their ownership of unique lifestyle and luxury properties. I am inspired to bring transformation to real estate through my way of being. I feel blessed that I found a business that allows me to use everything I have ever learned in my life on a daily basis. I draw on my background as an award-winning filmmaker, my background in architectural design, and my education. Beyond the value added to your investment portfolio, real estate offers a wealth of experience unobtainable anywhere else.

Early in my career I took one of my clients to see what turned out to be an Ed Fickett home. My client had no experience in midcentury architecture and, like many people in Southern California, had no idea who Fickett was or all that he had accomplished. As a native Angeleno, I know a lot about local architects. I studied architecture in college and consider myself to be a midcentury geek. Ed Fickett was called the "Frank Lloyd Wright of the 1950s" by *Better Homes and Gardens.* As an advisor to President Eisenhower, Fickett shaped housing policy in America. He grew up in Beverly Hills and returned after his military career to design homes in Southern California, often on land that others rejected as unbuildable. His designs take advantage of Southern California's amazing weather by seamlessly integrating outdoor and indoor living spaces with open floor plans, energetic rooflines, high ceilings, open beams, and glass walls.

The property we looked at had been owned by the same person for 30 years. At some point the owner had decided to cover up 13 clear story windows, giving the home a more generic ranch house feel. This offered an amazing opportunity for the right buyer. The house was selling for under a million dollars and fit the profile of what my client was looking for—he wanted at least a 2,000-square-foot home with a minimum of three bedrooms and two bathrooms. I said to my client, "You have no idea what we just walked into: a house with pedigree. The house will feel bigger and brighter when the windows are uncovered. It will have that cool Palm Springs vibe." At a time when properties were selling with 12 or more offers, this home had only had one other offer. It was priced well below the market. It was an incredible deal.

We submitted an offer that was below the asking price and it was accepted. At the close of escrow, the work began to transform the property by honoring the original architect's intent and enhancing it to today's standards. Like Michelangelo's David, the work of art was trapped inside the property and the figure was released by carefully chiseling away. When we were done with the property, the owner had spent a couple hundred thousand dollars on improvements, transforming a $1.135 million-investment into one worth $2 million. But that wasn't the only transformation I witnessed. My client now lived in a home with pedigree, and I experienced his personal transformation from merely happy to experiencing true joy. This home has become an important part of my client's life. If it were to come on the market today would fetch nearly $3 million—but it is not for sale.

This client had a vision for what he wanted his home lifestyle to be. The opportunity I had was to help him discover what was possible with the resources he had available to invest by offering my perspective, capabilities, and architecture, design, and building experience. Clients rely on our team for cutting-edge branding and marketing strategies that increase the profile and prospective sale price of every property we sell. Every property has a story to be told. With our Hollywood storytelling experience, we get the right messaging to potential buyers. The story of the property can be told with a big opening, expansive shots, an emotional soundtrack, and a memorable ending.

One memorable property that we sold during the recession was positioned in just such a manner. We created anticipation for the listing through our marketing, so that the day of the launch we had more than 300 people tour the home leading to seven offers. Beyond the traditional and digital marketing kits, it was the relentless commitment to win for our client's experience—and to overcome in what we all knew was one of the most challenging real estate environments in recent history. The *Los Angeles Times* named this property as a Home of the Week. We were able to command a premium for this A. Quincy Jones property that always had a special place in my heart. Yes, because of my love for iconic properties but much more importantly for who I would meet there.

Entering the A. Quincy Jones home through an enormous 12-foot door is how I got the first glimpse of the woman that would become my wife. One evening, as the door opened our eyes met for the first time and Cupid's arrow struck our hearts. Our lives were transformed through real estate. Our mutual friend Linda had suggested to both of us that we should meet because she thought that we would hit it off. Linda saw something as it was and had the vision to see what it could be. My wife and I have now been married for more than 9 years and have forged a partnership in our personal and business lives to create St. James + Canter Luxury Real Estate.

After we were married, Linda eventually moved to Los Angeles and we used our gift to find her a fantastic home. When Linda's daughter moved here, we were able to find her a condo. When Linda's mother wanted to move to Los Angeles, we found her a condo, too. A week after she moved in she decided to sell. Although she had only owned the property for a week when we listed it, we sold the condo for a profit. When the daughter also decided to sell, we positioned her property to sell for a substantial profit. This is just one example of how we cultivate multigenerational client experiences through the family partnerships that are created in our extraordinary service experience. Our clients refer their friends and family to us because our service is an art—an art in representation, presentation. and ease in achieving a seamless 150-point transaction experience.

I get great joy in being of service to people searching for homes and distinct properties. Experiencing that joy should motivate you to become a realtor, rather than the dollar signs. When you are building a team, you have the ultimate responsibility to inspire a sense of ownership akin to that of an extended family. The associates, vendors, and, most importantly, clients that I work with have become the fabric of my life.

The process with which I approach real estate is ingrained in my personality. I adopt clients into my family and internalize their hopes and dreams into the treasure hunt I conduct on their behalf. Their joy becomes my joy in seeing them realize their highest level of satisfaction from owning not just a piece of property but also the home that elevates their existence. When their circumstances change, I get the call to help them sell their treasure and I set about treasure hunting for the next custodian that will bring honor to and safeguard their lives. In both buying and selling, my holistic approach to my business touches on art, design, architecture, landscaping, and storytelling. My clients become my life-long partners.

Given the pedigree of the properties and services that we engage, many of our clients are ultra-high net worth billionaires. But we're proud to also represent first-time buyers that are scraping pennies together. One of my greatest accomplishments is selling my highest dollar property ever in Malibu and my lowest dollar value condo in West Hollywood in the same year. Both of the buyers felt that they were my only client. We gave them the same level of service because the monetary value of a transaction does not define the legacy impact of how people are treated. A real experience is often about two people building their lives, whether through buying or selling. I want to be part of growing with both people's lives.

The beauty of being a realtor with this philosophy—one of providing an extraordinary service experience—is that you don't sell just anyone anything. Instead, you provide opportunities for your clients to grow, and they do. Every one of my clients has grown in riches, wealth, and joy through their real estate investments. All of them have benefited because of our collaborations. And when your clients grow, you grow.

More than any other investment, homes transform people's lives. Buying the right property offers returns not just in appreciation in value but also in transformation of people's lives. I focus on that transformation—it is what gets me up every morning, because I know I make a difference. That brings fulfillment in my life. I don't deal simply in real estate transactions—I manage transformations. I am here to provide service that will enrich the quality of all of our lives: today, tomorrow, and into the future.

CHAPTER 12

PEACE OF MIND COSTS PENNIES

By **MICHAEL NAVARRE**

Ask anyone who's received a claim check from their insurance company if they spent too much on their policy—I guarantee they'll say no. I've seen many clients get insurance payouts—some in the six figures—and have yet to hear any of them tell me they spent too much on insurance. In fact, they've spent pennies in relation to the dollars received.

I once had a company client who had an investment property that burned down in a fire; his claim payout was substantial. He felt changes in the neighborhood and property values made it less interesting to rebuild—so he looked to do other things with claim payout funds. He took that money to buy his own insurance business–a Farmers Insurance agency.

This illustrates a point: the best part of insurance is the fact that the money paid back to you from claims is yours to keep and you can use it for anything you like, from rebuilding to moving, funding retirement or investing in a business.

As much as it's your choice on how to spend insurance proceeds, you also have a choice on how much you pay for insurance premiums. Every client–every person–is unique and special, which means their choices for insurance should also be unique and special. This chapter will focus on how you–the client– can get your insurance to do what serves you the best. It's my belief that insurance is the financial instrument that gives you unlimited upside potential in your property, with us shouldering the downside risk. Property insurance is the best bargain that comes from using other people's money. After reading this chapter, I hope that you learn two things: What to ask for, and how to spend efficiently on what matters.

The Best Insurance Question

In California, we have a tightly regulated insurance market with common contracts offered across many carriers. Still, there is so much variation and choice that it can be difficult to know with confidence that you have covered the risks to your property. To know with confidence about these risks and the various coverages, you'd pretty much have to learn enough to be a licensed insurance professional. Instead I encourage you to seek out an experienced agent and ask the following questions:

- What are all the things that can possibly happen to my building?

- Have you covered them?

Any agent that is worth their salt will say: I don't know what can happen to your building. And I won't know if you have it covered until you and I have discussed it.

The agent would then start with the basics. These are called the perils that will cause damage. They include: fire, lightning, wind, hail, theft, vandalism, water damage, falling objects, flood, earthquake, ice and snow. The list goes on and on.

You could look at all of them and say, Ok, some of them I don't have to worry about. Ice and snow in Southern California? I won't worry about that. But earthquakes? That I worry about.

You must decide: As a building owner, what level of risk am I willing to take? If you want to cover all of these perils, you'll pay a lot in insurance. If you want to assume some of the risk, you don't remove a coverage; rather, you increase a deductible.

This is an important point. Let's say you may not want, say, earthquake coverage, but you take the policy and with it a $50,000 deductible. You put a little bit of your money on the table. Where we are in Southern California, which is actually not as high a risk, as other areas like Texas or Florida, the cost of insurance will be, let's say, about $1,000 on a $500,000 building. That's about a penny to five dollars. It's going to take 500 years, and you're not going to live six lifetimes, long enough to pay enough premium to pay for that house.

Think about it: you buy a $5 Starbucks coffee every day of the year, which costs you $1,825. That's a homeowner's premium on a $1-million home here in Southern California. You can protect your entire investment in your home for that cup of Starbucks.

If you ask the right questions, you'll soon figure out if you are getting the best insurance coverage for your needs. Understanding the policy coverage limits will also avoid being underinsured. While it can be tempting to have lower limits, it would be costlier if it comes to a claim.

A common mistake people make is to underinsure a building. Let's say you bought it 20 years ago and paid only $200,000 for it. Well that building in Los Angeles County can be worth $2 million now. In the event you have a small claim—for a partial loss—you're not going to get paid anything for it. Or you may not have ordinance of law, and you have a partial claim, but you will be required to get the building up to current ordinances without the coverage available to pay for it.

Here's what happens with underinsurance. Let's say the building is worth $100,000 and you can insure it for 80 percent or more of its value—so $80,000. But you don't have any money into the property, so you say you want to insure it for $50,000. You can legally do that. State law says if you have a partial claim—let's say a $20,000 fire claim, because you only insured 50 percent of the building—you are only going to get 50 percent of your money, less your deductible. So take $20,000, multiply it by half and that's $10,000, minus a $1,000 deductible. You'll only get $9,000 for your loss.

The average consumer doesn't know this 80 percent coinsurance rule, and it can put you out of business.

Another way to get stuck is to not protect yourself from the catastrophe that you don't think will happen. In Los Angeles people say, if the big one happens the government will come and bail us out. The government isn't going to come bail you out: You need earthquake insurance.

Keith Wagner owns a Farmers Insurance agency in Texas and gives 50 seminars a year on insurance. He lives in Houston, which encountered devastating losses from Hurricane Harvey in 2017. "No one expected 53 inches of rain," said Wagner. "Even as it was happening at my house we had 39 inches. We had people that were high and dry in every other storm that are now out of business. There are entire neighborhoods that have to be torn down."

He said, "I'm willing to bet that the vast majority do not have earthquake coverage, that over two-thirds to three-fourths do not have earthquake insurance in Southern California. In an area where your number one risk is earthquake. It's not lightning. It's not fire. It's not if it will happen. It's when it will happen. It could happen in the next 10 minutes. Or in 10 years. We don't know." It's actually worse than Wagner predicted: five out of six people do not have earthquake insurance as of 2017.

Insurance Saving Strategies

Making poor insurance choices can cost you hundreds of dollars in the short term (bad enough), but those choices may actually cost you thousands of dollars and a great deal of stress in the long term. If you choose insurance just because it is cheap, you often overlook the right coverage amount or how you will be paid in a claim.

Do some research about credible home insurance carriers in your area, and don't wait until the last minute to make a decision. You don't want to feel pressured to make a choice quickly, and you will save money by carefully considering the coverages you get with your home policy.

In considering how to save on insurance coverage, here's my number one tip: figure out what your pain point is, and that's your deductible. If you have the money on hand and are willing to pay for damages resulting from a claim, then you can increase your deductible to the maximum amount you're financially able to afford if something happens right now and you have to pay for it immediately. Whether it is $500, $1,000, or $5,000 more than the minimum deductible, if you are financially comfortable, then take the savings your insurance company will give you and start saving money.

Usually it will take you five to seven years to make back the deductible in your savings. That's a good rule of thumb for a building owner. There are a lot of people that have a $1,000 deductible on a multi-million-dollar building. Why do that? You're not going to make a $1,000 claim. Put in a $10,000 deductible. If some glass is broken, you'll just call out the glass vendor and get it done.

Having said that, the less money you have, the more important it is to have insurance to protect you if something goes wrong. If you are struggling to come up with money to pay for your insurance, you may want to think twice about increasing your deductible. A caring advisor who has gotten to know your personal situation is going to be your friend in navigating this decision.

To find best available discount offers, here's my second tip: insurance companies are like most businesses, with points of differentiation that will make their offerings most attractive to their target clients. Getting carriers to offer discounts is not automatic; it usually takes research and bundling of multiple policies with the same carrier. If you don't take advantage of bundling your home and car insurance, you will pay more for home insurance than someone who puts all their insurance with one company.

Evaluate the total cost of both policies with the same insurer. If you look at the total cost of insurance, your car insurance might be more expensive with your home insurer, but the discount you get on your home insurance may make the total cost of your insurance less. Always evaluate your insurance as an entire package and not one-on-one. Be strategic and use all your policies to negotiate the best price.

A lot of people worry that if they cancel their policy before the renewal date, they will get hit with a penalty for canceling. What most people don't realize is that if you are canceling a policy mid-term or before your insurance renewal to save money or get more coverage, it actually pays to cancel your policy early.

This year, a client came to me with a home insured by carrier A, cars by carrier B, earthquake coverage by carrier C, umbrella liability by carrier D, and a collector car by carrier E. Everything was on separate bills, and each came due at different times. After our review and consolidation, some of the insurance premiums were trimmed by half; this client got even more risks covered for higher limits and the premiums were reduced by thousands of dollars a year.

I already mentioned the best question you should ask your agent, but here's the best question an agent should ask you: "Why do you want insurance?"

I can learn so much about my client by how they answer that question. It helps me connect with their concerns and hopes. I care deeply for my clients, as if they were family, and by understanding them better I can step into their shoes to see things from their perspective and offer coverage as if I was getting it for myself.

Our agency motto—which is engraved on the wall at the entrance—says: "The measure of our worth is not what we have done to help ourselves, but what we have done to help others."

If your insurance person has done their job, you'll be enjoying peace of mind and you'll be positioned for prosperity.

CHAPTER 13

HOW YOU CAN LEVERAGE YOUR SEO EFFORTS TO MAXIMIZE SHORT TERM RESULTS

By **NABIL JALIL**

First of all, it's important to understand the fundamentals of how search engines work. According to the traditional explanation, the two components that search engines will use to determine if your business will be listed at the top of their search results relates to what you have on and off your website.

This is commonly known as on-page and off-page factors.

On-page factors are connected to the 'backend' of a website. This is where SEO experts optimize the coding, content, and structure of a website to better conform to the standards of Google's algorithm. We do this by creating sitemaps, adding schema, adding alt tags and geo-location in pictures, while also updating title tags and headings that focuses on the keywords most likely to lead to the site.

On the other hand, off-page factors deal with the quality of links that are connected to your website as well as social shares connected to your business, the type of traffic that lands on your website and many other factors. This component ultimately focuses on the digital footprint that your website has all over the internet.

Although both of these components contribute to your website's ability to gain more exposure in the search engines, the amount of weight that is placed on each is generally dependent on how easily they can be manipulated or falsely manufactured.

Therefore, we will be focusing on two factors that are hard to manipulate and manufacture. Through our research, this will not only contribute the most to your SEO efforts, but it will also help you achieve your end goal, to acquire more clients as soon as possible.

These two factors are earned links and targeted non-search engine traffic.

Before going over these factors in more detail, we must refocus our definition on how search engines work to better understand why you should be prioritizing both of these factors during an SEO campaign.

At their core, search engines will evaluate your website based on the number of trusted and powerful people you have built relationships with and are talking about your business in a positive way.

How that translates into SEO terminology is quite simple; The number of trusted and powerful people that are talking about your business is considered to be the number of websites that are linking back to yours and that have a strong online presence.

These types of links, also commonly known as backlinks, are the foundation that search engines are built on because each link is a form of referral.

The more that trusted and powerful people are talking about your website in a positive way, the greater the implication that you are delivering a high-quality service or product. Otherwise, why would they want to mention your business to their followers?

Google started to use links, as the main basis to determine how well a website should be ranked because links are similar to regular, word of mouth referrals. Before the internet, most people would talk with each other to spread news of good quality businesses.

People would say things like *"Hey this guy is awesome for this service."* Or, *"This company is great, but this company is better."* These conversations were used as a way to gauge the quality of a business.

Now, in the modern internet age, it is all about links. Links are simply people that are talking about businesses through word of mouth, but online. And it's this process that helps build your website's online authority and relevance in the eyes of search engines.

Acquiring relevance and authority through the lens of Google's search engine Artificial Intelligence (AI), known as Rank Brain, is essential for any website. There are millions of websites on the internet; when someone searches a specific keyword, you want yours to be visible before all the rest.

Rank Brain essentially manages the algorithm that will sift through sites using "crawlers" in order to figure out the quality of a website. Since Google's goal is to provide the best websites for their users, Rank Brain updates itself regularly to avoid giving high visibility to low quality websites.

Each time Google rolls out new updates, they become more ruthless in evaluating a website before it can be put on their best search results.

In the past, numerous low-quality websites were spammed to garner the fastest and highest rankings. After Google released the Penguin algorithm update in 2012, links became vetted in the strictest way possible.

The Penguin update was groundbreaking when it launched, and it has only become more sophisticated over time. The algorithm cracks down on a variety of obvious unnatural backlink patterns.

Google will never release the full details of their algorithm updates. But based on research, there are 3 main backlink factors that can be used to identify unnatural link patterns: link quality, link velocity, and link diversity. Today we will focus solely on link quality because you can implement it right after you finish reading this chapter without the help of an SEO expert.

What is the easiest way for Google to determine a quality of the link? The traffic or "referrals." Real traffic is the hardest thing to manipulate, and most of the time, only real and established businesses and websites have traffic.

This assertion is also backed up by Google patents that mention the importance of traffic in their algorithms as a way to grade a website's authority and relevance; more specifically on the amount of traffic generated by each link.

The concept of earning a link is based on a relationship development process between you and a digital entity. You contribute some form of value to them as a form of incentive to link out or talk about your business, in return, you will be able to leverage their followers and drive them to your website.

This strategy focuses on finding authorities in your marketplace that have your clients and building online relationships with them to create short-term opportunities.

This link and relationship building strategy not only helps you gain coveted rankings in search results, but also helps you build great business relationships with owners of websites within the real estate industry. This saves you time and resources while you build your business–killing two birds with one stone.

One of the best ways you can get links from an SEO standpoint is through your content. Well how can you determine what type of content to publish? That depends on the needs of those prospects you hope will provide you with links.

The first step of this relationship building process is to identify and connect with your direct client or with authorities in the real estate marketplace that have access to your direct clients. To determine who you should be investing your time with, it is essential to evaluate how much each prospect is worth.

The best metric to use is how much traffic or followers they have access to. With respect to your prospects website, they must have a decent amount of paid and organic traffic to it. After that, you would need to research those prospective websites to have a better understanding about their expectation and needs to determine the best angle to approach and contact them. This step is the research phase.

Throughout this process, you will be gathering information to have a better understanding of your prospect and its target audience and clients. This will help you figure out the way to provide value to both of these targets.

At the end of the day, the main question that needs to be answered is what their needs are and how can you build relational equity with them which is the last and third step to this process.

Relational equity is the value of your relationship with the prospect. You can start building it right away as you are reaching out to them with simple messages such as "hey, I wrote this really good piece of content and I want to share it with you because your audience might find it interesting."

It can not only add tremendous value to them but also increase the chances of them sharing it with their followers or wanting to learn more about what you do. You just have to make sure that there is a need for this content based on your research.

Unfortunately, most of the time, this one interaction is not enough and more relational equity has to be built before the prospect feels comfortable linking to your website and sharing your business to their network. Therefore, it is highly recommended to build relational equity first before trying to obtain a link from your prospect.

To build relational equity, you need to engage with your prospect online and interact with any online property they have. Leaving a comment on their blog, liking a social media post or joining their LinkedIn group and answering any of the member's questions, will all help you build relational equity. Once your prospect is aware of you and you have provided value using these approaches; it's time to figure out how to get a link from them.

The purpose of going over this 3-step process is to emphasize the importance of having a systemized approach to building your list of prospects and an online relationship with them before going for the ask.

This will significantly increase your closing rate mainly because your prospects will already "know you" and as long as you have provided some form of value to them, you can take advantage of the reciprocity principle which simply means that your prospects will feel like they owe you something after you've helped them out.

Below is an example on how to put this 3-step process into action if you were a real estate lawyer. This method is also applicable for any real estate professionals or firms. All you need to do is reverse engineer the steps tailored to your specific goals or needs:

1. Identify and Connect

There are multiple online platforms that you can use to find your prospects but before anything, we would highly recommend you make a list of the different types of prospects you would like to do business with and the different locations you can provide your services.

For this example, let's say that our main targets are multi-family property managers in Los Angeles.

The next step is to identify your prospects by searching for "multi-family property managers in Los Angeles" on all major online channels such as Google, LinkedIn, Twitter, Facebook, etc... and adding them to a list.

Look for their website, social media properties and if they have any social media groups and add all of this information to your list.

Do not only limit yourself to businesses. Look for associations, blogs, influencers, educational institutions and any other organizations that can give you access to many of your clients.

Once you have built out your list of prospects, you need to be able to prioritize them on a purely quantitative level and there are multiple metrics that can be used such as:

- The value of organic traffic to their website

- The value of paid traffic to their website

- Number of social media followers, subscribers, etc.

- The size of your prospect's social media groups

From an SEO standpoint, the first two metrics mentioned above should be the primary factor to evaluate a link-building prospect however, you should not limit your research to this because you can leverage the other online platforms to drive qualified traffic to your website right away.

Once you have prioritized each of your prospects, the next step is to start connecting with them by:

- Subscribing to their newsletter

- Liking their Facebook business page

- Following the business on Twitter

- Adding the owner to your LinkedIn network and following their LinkedIn page

- Joining their LinkedIn group

- Etc...

It's important to understand that it takes around 7-15 touches before turning a lead into a qualified prospect.

The purpose of this step is to start creating these touches and increasing the likelihood of your prospects being aware of you and your business.

2. Research and monitor

The purpose of this section is to research each of your prospects and monitor their online activity, so you have enough information to have a better understanding on their needs and goals.

For example, if you subscribed to their newsletter, what are they trying to accomplish with it?

- Are they trying to get more subscribers?

- Are they promoting other businesses?

- Are they trying to sell anything?

This step is important because it will give you enough information to figure out how you can provide them value and the best angle to approach and ask them for something without seeming needy or selfish.

3. Building Relational Equity

As previously mentioned, there are multiple ways to build relational equity with your prospects.

The easiest way is to engage with their social media profiles by liking their posts, sharing and commenting on them.

However, the amount of value they will be getting is not based on the actual action but more so on their benefit from that action.

If you are sharing a post to your followers and you only have 5, the benefit that your prospect will receive out of this is very low.

But if you had a large following, the benefit for your prospect will be much greater. Especially if you let them know and can quantify the impact...

Another great way to provide value is by sharing information that can help them with a specific situation they might be dealing with.

During the research phase, if you found a post mentioning that they are facing challenges that relate to a specific law, you can provide some clarity or guidance using your content or sharing someone else's.

These 3-steps should be continuously implemented throughout your SEO campaign if you want to keep your pipeline full of link-building prospects.

When the opportunity presents itself, the final step is to ask for something in return.

For example, if you found out about a new real estate law in Los Angeles that is coming into effect very soon, you should write an article about it on your website.

Once this is done, you should reach out to your prospects.

Tell them about this law and that it could be very valuable for their newsletter subscribers if, based on your research, they promote this type of content in their newsletters.

You should also ask them if they don't mind mentioning (or linking to) your post on their website so all their users can also be aware of it.

And to fully maximize the return on your article, you should start promoting it to prospects that are your direct clients or that have access to them such as property management associations, real estate magazines, news outlets, etc.

This chapter is meant to serve as a crash-course and guide to start your very own online marketing endeavors through SEO. I encourage you to revisit the steps that were laid out and ask yourself: "How can I make it work in my business?" Instead of saying: "This is too complicated" or "This is too simple and might not work for me because...."

Ultimately, SEO is still all about closing deals and making more money for your business. It is a vehicle for you to leverage in growing your business to the next level. The visibility and traffic that you gain during the later stages of your SEO campaign will definitely give you more opportunities in closing sales.

But now, with the information presented in this chapter, you are well equipped to go out there and get significant quick results for your business while your investment in SEO comes to fruition down the road. Take the leap and reap the rewards!

CHAPTER 14

THE LEGAL RISKS OF INVESTMENT PROPERTIES

By **RAY KERMANI**

Last week I received an all too familiar call from one of my real estate clients: "I just bought this income property for a great deal. The numbers and aesthetics looked perfect on paper. But now I can't raise the rent, I can't change the tenants, the city is constantly inspecting my units, I am being sued by tenants for events that happened years ago, and the city won't let me redevelop my units without spending an enormous amount of money and time on permits, inspections, and a $20,000 relocation fee per unit to move out the tenants."

Even if you purchase what appears to be the perfect investment property on paper, legal risks could turn the investment upside down quickly. In my experience, income property, particularly in highly regulated large suburban cities, such as San Francisco, New York, and Los Angeles, comes with too many strings attached, which management companies and investors seldom understand. In this chapter, I answer some of the most common questions relating to investment properties. The goal of this chapter is to help make it easier for investors and landlords to fulfill the dreams they had when first buying income properties: increased wealth and reduced headaches.

Do I need a property management company to maximize my revenue from income properties?

The simple answer is no. In fact, management companies often expose landlords to unnecessary risks and expenses. Among my colleagues, I am considered one of the premier landlord-tenant attorneys in Los Angeles, which has some of the most complicated housing laws in the country. I have represented hundreds of landlords and property management companies and have successfully litigated dozens of unlawful detainer (evictions) cases to jury verdict, and hundreds more prior to verdict. Although these victories are sweet, they are incredibly expensive, and often result in uncollectable judgments against bankrupt tenants.

I have also sued landlords and management companies for negligence and premises liability. These experiences have taught me two important facts: that property management companies are very easy targets to sue, and that one bad lawsuit can turn a real estate investment into a nightmare. The key is to assemble a strong legal team that prevents catastrophe instead of the old-fashioned method of sloppy management followed by expensive litigation. A simple analysis by the right attorney of a building and its tenants prior to purchase can make the difference between a high performing asset and a money-drain.

What do management companies do wrong and do I need one?

Property management is a multi-billion-dollar industry. Yet those working in property management don't undergo any formal training. Although real estate brokers are required to pass a licensing exam in order to manage a property, a license to buy and sell real estate does not prepare anyone for the legal tsunami that a bad property creates. Property management is a highly competitive industry that emphasizes taking short-term cuts to increase short-term gains, but often these shortcuts lead to monumental losses. We've had clients spend tens of thousands of dollars on legal fees because they didn't want to spend $50 on a registered process server at the outset or because they didn't want to credit a tenant $25 in late fees. The key is to implement sound policies that balance the need for immediate profit while safeguarding against long-term losses. The good news is that landlords can have their proverbial cake and eat it, too, so long as they use the right recipe when making a purchase. After a purchase is made, it is important to implement sound policies and practices that are profitable and also minimize litigation risk.

Management companies often make mistakes while operating a building. Common mistakes include: failing to maintain tenant files, failing to maintain proper accounting practices, charging illegal or excessive late fees, failing to conduct proper move-in and move-out inspections, hiring inexperienced staff, failing to provide non-

English speaking tenants with translated notices and agreements when necessary, improperly serving notices, and so on. Cutting corners usually backfires in real estate, especially in rent-controlled cities.

There is no need to hire a property management company if you assemble a strong internal management team and hire competent counsel that can advise at the outset on the best business and legal practices. For example, in 2014 my law firm, Kermani LLP, represented one of the largest real estate investment companies in Los Angeles. Let's refer to them as Acme. Acme owned a billion-dollar portfolio of more than 10,000 units throughout the country. In 2014, the client purchased a 50-unit building in the city of Los Angeles. The property had a history of extensive litigation, including multiple lawsuits for inadequate housing conditions and a class action lawsuit. The building was targeted for seven years by a tenant-side law firm that had a reputation for terrorizing landlords. Acme was convinced that given its extensive background in real estate and large financial portfolio, the problems presented would be easy to deal with.

Upon purchasing the property, all but a handful of tenants instituted a rent strike and refused to pay rent for nearly a year. The building manager, who failed to carry out the most basic of tasks during his tenure as manager, joined the rent strike. The former manager also filed an employment lawsuit against Acme, which hired our firm to remedy the entire disaster only after other eviction and employment law firms failed to fix the situation. Our firm filed eviction actions against both the ringleader of the tenants and the former property manager. After we secured victories against these two, the entire building capitulated and agreed to a favorable settlement for the client. The building was vacated. Prior to our involvement, Acme spent hundreds of thousands of dollars on expensive lawyers and insurance deductibles without any success and with no end in sight. To make matters worse, the lawyers hired by Acme's insurance company to defend against the tenants' lawsuits recommended that Acme hold off on evicting any of the tenants. As everyone knows, possession is nine-tenths of the law and the most critical piece of leverage in a landlord-tenant dispute. The key to success is to be proactive in preventing a lawsuit and proactive in aggressively prosecuting an action once litigation is inevitable. The best way to be proactive is to bring in litigation specialists, people who have fought dozens of courtroom battles and can predict from first-hand experience what will happen down the road if the right steps aren't taken from the beginning.

Why is the Eviction Process So Complicated?

Many of you may wonder: Why was the eviction process so complicated for Acme? Why is it so difficult for other landlords in Los Angeles? The simple answer is: Rent control laws and eviction jury trials. Most lawyers across the country, and even many lawyers in California, have never heard of an eviction jury trial or the horror stories of rent control.

All multi-unit residential dwellings built prior to 1979 in the City of Los Angeles are subject to the Los Angeles Rent Stabilization Ordinance. Many major U.S. cities, such as New York, San Francisco, Oakland, and Boston also enforce rent control laws which limit the amount that rent can increase per year for a unit, and prevent a landlord from evicting a tenant "just because." Do you ever wonder why some residents in Santa Monica pay $1,200 per month to rent a two-bedroom, two-bathroom apartment one block from the ocean? The answer is rent control. It is very difficult, expensive, and occasionally impossible to evict rent-controlled tenants. To relocate rent-controlled tenants, you have to prove to the city that you have valid grounds for relocation (e.g., owner-occupancy), obtain approval from the city, and pay relocation fees upwards of $20,000 per unit.

Additionally, in some states, such as California, all tenants are entitled to a jury trial for an unlawful detainer case. This means that a rent controlled tenant, who pays $600 per month in rent, can force a landlord to spend tens of thousands of dollars on legal fees to evict a tenant in a week-long jury trial. For those of you who have never experienced a jury trial, it is in fact very similar to a courtroom television drama. A legal team has to appear for several days in front of a judge and jury to prosecute a case proving the landlord is entitled to possession.

In addition, because eviction proceedings require a landlord to follow the eviction statutes strictly, a landlord could easily lose an eviction case because of a technical error in their management of a tenant's file. For instance, if a landlord serves a notice demanding 50 cents more rent than permissible under the local rent control law, the landlord loses. The landlord could also end up paying the tenant's legal fees if there is a provision in the lease providing for such fees. This means that the $600 per month tenant, who is six months delinquent in rent, now gets to live in the unit for another six months rent free, plus the landlord has to pay the tenant's $10,000 in legal fees. Landlords should always "measure twice and cut once," as the saying goes.

Should I Invest in Commercial or Residential Property?

There is a myth that commercial real estate is a safer investment than residential real estate for two reasons: (1) commercial tenants are supposed to be sophisticated business owners that will pay their rent on time and care for the property better than residential tenants; and (2) commercial evictions are easier than residential evictions. Although there is some truth to this statement, it all depends on where the property is located and what the terms of the lease are. Commercial property is largely immune from the stringent and tenant-friendly laws that protect residential tenants. However, commercial real estate is often far more difficult to rent, especially in an internet-driven retail world where Amazon continues to increase its market capitalization, and many retail businesses fail. Moreover, commercial leases are often lengthy and convoluted, which make the management and eviction process expensive. We've represented both landlords and tenants in nightmarish commercial eviction trials that drag on for more than a year because the landlord failed to carefully draft the lease agreement or because the landlord chose the wrong attorney to prosecute the eviction. On the flipside, many of our clients have amassed millions of dollars from prudent real estate investments. We recommend real estate investment only when presented with a high-value, low-risk property.

Can a Good Lease Mitigate Risk?

Yes. At least, in part. Drafting an ironclad lease agreement can substantially decrease the risk inherent in owning real estate. Further, both a transactional attorney and a genuine litigator should draft your lease agreement. Otherwise, you run the risk of including provisions in your lease agreement that are unenforceable. For example, one of my longtime colleagues is a real estate transactional lawyer at one of the largest and most prestigious law firms in the United States. He once asked me to review a lease agreement that included a waiver of the right to jury trial for a prospective tenant. What he didn't know was that a landlord cannot waive a tenant's constitutional right to a trial by jury. Landlord leases commonly include a clause entitling only the landlord to attorneys' fees in the event that a dispute arises with a tenant. However, the law makes any attorneys' fees clause mutual, which means that regardless of what the lease says, if the tenant wins the case, the tenant will also get attorneys' fees if the lease entitles the landlord to recover his or her fees. As a practical matter, attorneys' fees clauses almost never make business sense for the landlord since tenants who fail to pay rent often lack the assets to satisfy a monetary judgment. A well-drafted lease is not a silver bullet but it will protect landlords from most harms. Our firm is well versed in these issues because our law firm consistently litigates the most complex lease provisions at trial.

Late Fees, Common Area Dues, and Rent Increases

Landlords often increase profits by charging late fees, issuing rent increase notices, and demanding common area dues. However, late fees are not always enforceable and are usually cost prohibitive to enforce in court. To solve this dilemma, we've helped our clients implement policies that allow them to enjoy the benefits that late fees offer while also eliminating the threat of loss caused by a late fee that's ruled illegal by a court.

In residential real estate, landlords must follow strict timelines and notice requirements when they want to increase the rent. In rent-controlled jurisdictions, rent increases are usually capped at 3 percent per year. A landlord must base common area dues upon actual and reasonable expenditures. If a landlord fails to comply with these rules, he or she could face serious legal consequences. For example, I once had a client who purchased a property in 2013. In 2002, the prior landlord had increased the annual rent by 5 percent. This means that the rent increases from 2002 through 2013 were illegal in every unit. As a result, the landlord had to reset the rents to every unit back to the 2002 rate. Thus, what began as a profit of $8,000 per month turned into a loss of hundreds of thousands of dollars. And the tenants' leases could not be terminated because the property was rent controlled. Had the landlord invested a couple of hours more during the due diligence period, he would have saved himself from such a calamitous transaction.

What Are the Most Common Legal Issues I Should Keep in Mind?

Housing laws, particularly in large metropolitan cities, are complicated. Landlords get sued everyday throughout the country for race discrimination, disability discrimination, labor law violations (as they pertain to managers), defective conditions within the unit, toxic tort issues (mold, lead, asbestos, and other forms of poison), and unlawful business practices. Clear and specific property policies for your employees and tenants are the most important tool against expensive lawsuits. Policies setting forth how and when notices (including eviction notices) are served, how and when late fees are charged and collected, how and when maintenance is scheduled, the hours and rate of pay for all personnel (including onsite property managers), are just a few of the important policies every landlord should have in place when operating a property, and preferably before purchasing one.

Although it may seem so at first, real estate is not always the surest way to fulfill the American Dream. Bad tenants, negligent management practices, and government regulations and laws can easily turn seemingly lucrative property investments into a nightmare. You should always hire intelligent and experienced attorneys prior to making a purchase. You should also consult with attorneys in both the management and maintenance of investment properties you already own to avoid costly mistakes in the future. Do not rely upon past practices or the wisdom of management companies. If you do, you could easily end up in one of the countless litigation nightmares we've had to rescue our clients from over the years. You'll make our job easier and your wallets heavier in the long run.

CHAPTER 15

ADAPTATION IN A CHANGING MARKET:
How to Deliver Extraordinary Returns to Ordinary Investors in Any Market

By **SCOTT A. CHAPLAN**

My first real estate acquisition was a three bedroom, two-bathroom condo in Tarzana, California. I was twenty-four years old. Being armed only with tenacity and a lack of fear of the unknown—easy since I didn't know what I didn't know. What I didn't have was credit, enough cash for the down payment, and income. I was in my early 20s and in my second year of law school. I simply didn't want to pay rent to someone else.

I needed 20 percent down and had only 10 percent. I needed to demonstrate income to obtain the institutional first trust deed. I thought I needed credit. At that juncture, I started thinking creatively (a gift from my dear, recently departed father). I found two law school friends to become tenants in the property I was yet to own. I took that income to the bank, and miraculously, they made me the loan conditioned upon my ability to find the 20 percent down payment. If you try to jump the Grand Canyon on a motorcycle, travel the mile width but miss the smooth landing by only one inch, you still end up a mile down at the bottom. I only had enough cash to clear half the chasm. With more bravado than sense, I pushed the seller, who achieved their exit price, to carry back 10 percent or find someone who would make that loan. I ended up owning that property for nearly 15 years, rented it out, earned profit, achieved a meaningful write off (at the time), and sold it at a gain. The goal didn't transcend my capacity but rather my experience; I learned the value of fellowship. Surrounding myself with those more knowledgeable than myself, I learned that "no" is a "yes" in disguise, hiding because the question wasn't properly presented (see **www. vowofprosperity.com**).

Shortly thereafter, I acquired 19 units, 36 units, and then 24 units. In each instance, these acquisitions transcended my personal capacity but never my tenacity. I've learned that the winner is always the one who gets up off the mat. That truism has carried me throughout my career. Today, after thousands of units, houses, commercial properties, and developments, it remains the fulcrum in a field where historians often attempt to predict the future—a difficult endeavor. Prudence; market knowledge; fundamentals; the willingness to accept, mitigate risk and intuition; in addition to tenacity and an unwillingness to stop or fail; continue to form my investment and business practices; and have led me and our team at DRU to our current success and inflection point in this changing market.

The Jobs Act

The Jumpstart Our Business Startups ("JOBS") Act was written in early 2012 and signed into law by President Barack Obama on April 5, 2012. Its intention was to spur investment, largely by unaccredited investors, with drivers including job creation, macro-prosperity domestically, and access to investment opportunities previously unavailable to all but the wealthy. The meaningful provisions of the JOBS Act included the gravamen of Title II of the act relative to the Broker-Deal Exemption, and the ability to have a single-issue sell certain securities to unaccredited investors without limitation (Regulation D, Section 506) up to one million dollars per year. In 2015, this ceiling was raised to 50 million dollars.

The Fund Manager's Dilemma, Maximizing Investor Returns: Changing The Model, Customer Acquisition Cost in a Shifting and Competitive Market

Capital, at present, is abundant in the market. Pricing is reaching unprecedented levels in our core markets nationally, rents are at an all-time high, CAP rates are lower than interest rates (a material challenge for all investors), and the national pattern of economic gain is the longest consecutive period I've witnessed in my life (120 months is the record for our country; we are at over 90 months of consecutive growth now).

The traditional real estate investment fund has a two percent management fee for assets under management ("AUM"), a 20 percent carry as a participation in assets acquired by the fund (the

"Carry"), and an organizational fee traditionally set at one percent. Since most fund managers are financial engineers and not operators, the standard prism is fee generation which, in competitive markets, may prove antithetical to the interests of investors. By focusing on the Carry and mitigating fees wherever and however possible, we can remain profitable and provide higher, more stable returns for our investors. We accomplish this through vertical integration and pass the attendant savings on to our investors and consumers (investors who borrow from or co-invest with us). We also achieve profit goals through efficient execution of our projects resulting from managing the majority of the elements of the transaction.

The Transactional Value Chain

The more points we touch in the transactional value chain, the lower the incremental cost to our investors and consumers. Lower costs to each of these subsets equates to higher, more consistent, and risk-mitigated returns for our investors.

Brokerage

DRU Brokerage and its DRU Estates and DRU Commercial divisions afford us deal sourcing in-house and the ability to react quickly in a changing market (in addition to cost coverage and cash flow). Our two office boutique brokerage will end 2018 with more than 50 agents in a distinct construct the market has never seen. As investors and operators first, we have a better understanding of the value chain our clients need. As a key client, we manifest our expectations throughout the brokerage and train our DRU family accordingly.

Design by Consuela®

DRU Brokerage competitors are not eating their own cooking.

We source for ourselves, scope rehabilitation and value-add prospects for both commercial and residential opportunities and provide these skill sets and relationships to our third-party clients. Our in-house design is performed by Consuela, a principal who is vice-president of DRU Brokerage, managing director of its estates division, key residential sourcing and disposition agent. Our sell through velocity is enhanced for all of our clients as a consequence of our deep understanding of what it takes to ensure market adoption once a project is exposed.

Greene, Fidler & Chaplan, LLP
In-House General Counsel

I am a founding partner of Greene, Fidler & Chaplan, a family business office and real estate firm established in 1995. GFC acts as general counsel for the DRU Family of Funds and all affiliated entities in addition to many clients who own tens of millions of square feet of commercial and multi-family residential properties nationally and internationally. We are one of the most active firms in California in the landlord-tenant space, affording us a seat as thought leaders and first movers for our brokerage, management and investment arms. We also ensure less expensive, more comprehensive problem solving and documentation skills than our competition, who hire advisors as needed, work to bring them up to speed, and hope to achieve the cohesive fluidity our well-worn path affords.

Investment and Hybrid Funds

Real estate investing is capital intensive, and the risks can be substantial based upon capital reserves, timing, rate risk, deal risk, operator risk, political risk, macro-economic and geopolitical risk. Equity investors (the riskiest tranche of capital in the stack in terms of marshaling of assets) often watch the "paper evaporation" of their true equity during fluctuations or a material downturn. If they are short-term players, the natural ebbs and flows within our complex economic system could prove disastrous—as it did for many during the Great Recession of 2009 and 2010. Not every loss or impairment during a downturn is worthy of an admission of culpability by the investors damaged thereby. Both The Great Recession and the Great Depression resulted in systemic bank failures which left performing borrowers/investors without necessary funding despite the statutorily supported blatant breaches of the underlying loan agreements by the failing banks.

DRU is launching its hybrid funds to mitigate exposure to any single tranche in the capital stack, provide capital for sponsors we know and trust, and maintain their ability to turn the dial to ensure the ratio of debt to equity investments within the portfolio of our platform. Each investment we make, be it debt or equity, includes a portion of our own capital and, as a gating issue, is resonant within a deal we would prefer to own.

DRU's Virtual REIT® Crowdfunding Element

The decentralization of investment funding within the "fourth asset class," as real estate is here to stay. Some players are thriving and returning material quarterly results to their stakeholders, and others are chasing the burn rate associated with the profound investment in their platform technology, which has become more homogenous and cost effective. Our viewpoint is crowdfunding with the right operator from the optics of an investor can be a prudent move. It is not a technology play but rather an operator and cost of capital play.

The investor needs to understand the operator, their silo expertise, and ability to execute. Fancy reports don't pay bills; good investments do. Look at the spend on technology and marketing versus operational personnel when contemplating a home for your hard earned capital.

CAC is Back!

Operators need to drive down their cost of capital if they want to remain competitive and keep their promises to investors of being the right place for investment dollars in any economy. Times will change. Velocity in Southern California residential properties during the Great Recession fell drastically. The median sales price in LA County fell below $400k (compared to today's median of around $682k). Investors failed to timely pivot, and many were destroyed. Though costly, we survived.

Most crowdfunding sites contemplate a customer acquisition cost ranging from 8 to 12 percent. We lower that cost through the investment of our own funds, cross-marketing with our related entities and affiliates, and a more efficient spend. We are not velocity driven, and consequently, we do not need to chase investments in the equity tranche in a declining market. We also understand the debt placement timing, and the right sponsors with bridge capital needs allows us the diversity and allocation we need for risk mitigation during CAP rate compression, rising rates, narrowing LTV requirements, and traditional credit retraction climates. We are boarding agents weekly and accentuating their training to ensure preparedness for the upcoming reset that we predict will occur during the next two years.

I recently spoke at a conference in San Francisco and addressed Regulation A+ and our imminent participation in a new type of fundraising and investor base distribution. Both the participants and panelists confirmed my hypothesis relative to building the right team and ensuring your offering isn't merely a "for sale" sign in the desert. Without market makers, a firm underwriting commitment, a meaningful marketing budget, an execution team focused upon the fundamentals set forth above and an expanding relationship base, the best ideas fail. Our decision to broaden our bench, add placement agents, analysts, additional sourcing agents within our affiliated brokerage, and more management capacity is a reflection of the distinction between being smart and being wise. Experience has taught us that time to market, deployment velocity, sourcing the right deals—money can't cure a bad deal but instead can only delay the pain of failure—and running them hands-on remain mission-critical events that can counteract the extrinsic forces that will ultimately impact all markets.

Welcome to our third act. We hope you experience the joys of creation and participation while skipping some of the knee scraping that we survived over several decades. Today, we are thriving.

CONCLUSION

As a financial advisor, my clients come to me for conflict free advice that stewards them along their financial path in life. This book serves as a culmination of differing opinions and expertise. The aim of bringing these authors together was to create a resource that would help people navigate the real estate market. Real estate is and will likely remain a major component of investment portfolios both in the United States and abroad. When evaluating your investment plan it's important to get qualified individuals on your team. The following appendix lists the best route to contact the authors.

To your success,

Adam Torres

P.S. Don't forget to listen to the podcast, Money Matters Top Tips with Adam Torres, for ongoing up to date advice you can use. MoneyMattersTopTips.com/podcast

APPENDIX

Adam Torres | Chapter 1 | Page 1
Financial Advisor
MyInvestmentsMatter.com

Andrew Suzuki | Chapter 2 | Page 9
CEO of Suzuki Designs
SuzukiDesigns.com

Celestin Hariton | Chapter 3 | Page 17
CEO of Hariton Engineering
HaritonEng.com

Chirag Sagar | Chapter 4 | Page 25
COO of Destination Luxury
ChiragSagar.com

David Westley | Chapter 5 | Page 41
Registered Mortgage Broker

Jeff Neumeister | Chapter 6 | Page 51
CEO of Neumeister & Associates, Inc.
NeumeisterCPA.com

Joe Glaeser | Chapter 7 | Page 59
CEO of JMG Builders
JMGBuilder.com

John Fagerholm | Chapter 8 | Page 65
General Partner M.E.T.A.L. Law Group LLP
Founding Partner of Defend My Biz
MetalLawGroup.com
DefendMyBiz.com

Jorge Rabaso | Chapter 9 | Page 73
President of Rabaso Financial Protection
RabasoFinancial.com

Luis Guajardo | Chapter 10 | Page 83
Founder of Prive Luxury Rentals and Prive Travels
PriveLuxuryRentals.com

Markus Canter | Chapter 11 | Page 97
Founding Director New Homes Division at Berkshire
Hathaway HomeServices California Properties
Co-Founder, Partner St. James+Canter Luxury Real Estate
StJamesCanter.com

Michael Navarre | Chapter 12 | Page 105
Farmers® Agency Owner
Linkedin.com/in/MikeNavarre

Nabil Jalil | Chapter 13 | Page 113
Founder of BlackGrid SEO
BlackGridSEO.com

Ray Kermani | Chapter 14 | Page 127
Partner at Kermani LLP
Kermanillp.com

Scott Chaplan | Chapter 15 | Page 137
Founding Partner of Green, Fidler & Chaplan, LLP
Executive Chairman of Urban Group of Companies
GFCLLP.com
DelReyUrban.com

Listen to the

MONEY MATTERS
TOP TIPS PODCAST

where Business Owners, Entrepreneurs and Executives
share their top tips for success!

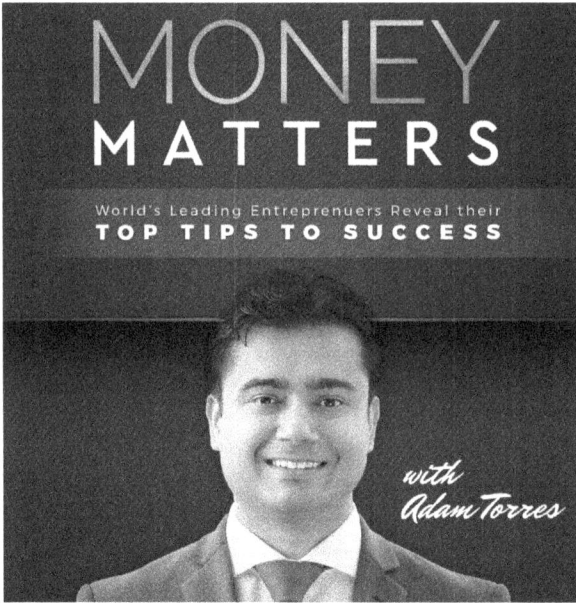

MoneyMattersTopTips.com/podcast

OTHER AVAILABLE TITLES

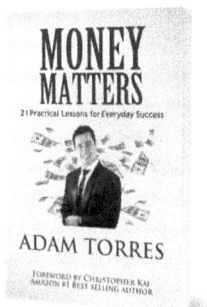

In this clear, concise manual, financial expert Adam Torres goes over the basics of personal finance and investing and shows you how to grow your wealth. Torres makes sure you are prepared for whatever life throws your way. It's never too early to think about the future and his book will give you the right tools to tackle it.

Purchase at **MoneyMattersTopTips.com/store** or listen to the audiobook version FREE on YouTube at Ask Adam Torres

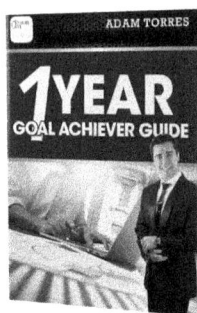

This workbook has been designed specifically for individuals like you who are dedicated to improving the results in all areas of their lives! By following the ideas and exercises presented to you in this transformational workbook, you are automatically moving yourself into the realm of top achievers worldwide.

Download FREE at **MoneyMattersTopTips.com/store**

www.ingramcontent.com/pod-product-compliance
Lightning Source LLC
Chambersburg PA
CBHW060603200326

41521CB00007B/651